Preaching the Gospel

by
Norman Pittenger
King's College
Cambridge

Morehouse-Barlow Co., Inc.
Wilton, Connecticut 06897

Morehouse-Barlow Co., Inc.
78 Danbury Road
Wilton, Connecticut 06897

ISBN 0-8192-1340-3

Library of Congress Catalog Card Number 83-62716

Printed in the United States of America

To
JOHN DRURY
Dean of Chapel
in King's College
and
Friend

Contents

Preface

THIS BOOK is a discussion of preaching, one of the central responsibilities of the ordained ministry of the Christian Church. Its concern is with what is sometimes called 'liturgical preaching', but I do not mean this in the narrower sense of preaching upon the appointed lections in the celebration of the Eucharist. Rather, I shall be considering preaching in a liturgical *context*, which is the celebration of the Eucharist on Sunday morning or at whatever time the main service of worship is conducted on the Lord's Day. Because of that particular focus, I shall not speak in this book of preaching on other occasions or in other contexts, although I am of course aware of the importance of such opportunities to proclaim the gospel. But in a brief study like this one it is impossible to say everything; I have thought it better to concentrate on preaching in the particular connection which I have indicated.

Preaching, like everything else within the Christian tradition, does not stand by itself alone. It requires an awareness of certain presuppositions, having to do with the nature of the Christian community to be sure but also with respect to the whole enterprise of religious faith. Anybody who has read other writings by me will know that for me the so-called 'Process' conceptuality provides the general presuppositions with which the entire Christian enterprise may most satisfactorily be approached in our own time. Hence I must begin with a chapter which looks at such presuppositions and will outline briefly and succinctly the way in which such a Process conceptuality understands what we are 'up to' in our Christian profession of faith and *a fortiori* what is for preaching the wider background of thought and understanding.

The chapters which follow take a line which ought to be clear enough: what it is that we preach; to whom we preach it; the setting of this preaching in worship; preachers and their responsibility; the relation of preaching to the biblical witness to and the ongoing tradition about the originating event of the Christian community; certain problems which we face in preaching today; the relationship of preaching to theology, which seeks to provide a consistent and coherent statement of faith's implications as well as the ethical consequences of the gospel that is proclaimed; and finally what I have called 'the end of preaching.' As to the last of these topics, I am using the word 'end' in both its senses: what is its basic purpose, on the one hand; and on the other hand the way in which all genuine preaching has its conclusion in the worship of God enacted in Jesus Christ.

Although my entire ministerial career has been spent in the teaching of ordinands, in theological colleges and seminaries and then in a university setting, I have been privileged to preach in many chapels, churches, and cathedrals over more than half-a-century. In doing this I have learned a good deal about what such preaching should intend and what it inevitably requires of the one who is asked to preach. I hope that this experience is reflected in what I have written. I hope also that what is said may be helpful to others to whom has been committed this exacting aspect of Christian ordained ministry.

Finally, I have written as a priest of the Anglican obedience and much but not all of what I say is naturally a reflection of that particular allegiance. But I do not think that this has narrowed my perspective nor that it has given it an insularly Anglican quality. Certainly I trust that this is not the case.

Much of my preaching in recent years has been in the Chapel of King's College in Cambridge, of which I am a member and in whose worship I take part almost every day. It is for that reason that I have ventured to dedicate this book to the present Dean of that Chapel. John Drury has been a good friend to me. So also have been his three predecessors with whom I have been associated: Alec Vidler, David Edwards, and Michael Till. I am grateful to all of them for much encouragement for more than the last twenty years.

Norman Pittenger

King's College
Cambridge

Preaching the Gospel

THE PROCLAMATION of Jesus Christ as Lord is basic to the life of the Christian community. What is more, preachers act for that community in their proclamation; they do not speak of themselves and for themselves. Recognition of this fact requires us to begin a discussion of presuppositions by speaking about the Church itself.

There are many different societies or groups in the world, all of which have some purpose or aim. Mutual help is one of these. Another is a sharing of common interests or objectives. Still another is the provision of opportunity for friendship or close association. But the Christian Church, which in some ways resembles such groups, has its own distinctive quality. To understand what that quality is, we need to consider two or three important points. One of them is that to which St. Paul pointed when he described the Christian community of his day as 'the Body of Christ.' By this he seems to have meant that the meaning of the Church was to be found in its acting so closely and directly for Jesus Christ and so significantly carrying on his work in the world that it was to him as our human body is to our human self.

It would be possible, but mistaken, to argue from this in an almost biological fashion. Indeed St. Paul appears to have done something of the sort when he speaks of the Church as Christ's body and those who belong to it by baptism as being members of that body. But we need not press the analogy too far, for if we do there is a danger that we shall make of the Church a substitute for the reality of the Lord himself, who is its head and principle of life, standing 'over it' (as we might say) both in mercy and in judgment. Nonetheless, the Church *is* so intimately the *Lord's* Church that it should be respected, honored, and esteemed. What is more, it is the indispensable means for making the reality of Christ a present factor in the ongoing world. Did it not exist, nothing significant could be known about him— even those who reject it are still dependent upon it for what can be known about that One from whom it took its origin.

Closely related to this meaning of the Church is another. The Christian fellowship is best understood as a living, developing, and dynamic tradition. Tradition, of course, can be interpreted in a dead and static way; but that is not the way in which the Church as tradition should be understood. As we shall see in a moment, the Church is a living 'social process', as I like to put it. In that respect it is like every other such process: it has an identity which is established by the very fact that it comes from the past which it unfailingly remembers; it lives in the present where its decisions and actions must be done; and it looks to the future where its purpose for existence will find fulfilment. So it is with every living organism; the Church is an instance, but a special one, of something that runs through the cosmos.

As such, the Church exists to make present in the contemporary world the event upon which it is built—the event of Jesus Christ, taken as of quite special importance in the affairs of the world. All its activity, of whatever kind, is intended to be an expression of that event and its significance. And its goal is the realization, so far as this may be accomplished in a world of space and time, of the deepest intention disclosed in the originating event.

If we rightly understand the point of God's action in the human existence of Jesus Christ and all that his existence implies, then we must say that the Church is the community in which God's active love is both disclosed and released into the world. So it was with the Lord himself. When the Church is true to its own true identity, it is the fellowship of those who have been caught up into and made participant in that divine Love made available for men and women of all sorts, classes, races, backgrounds, and experience. They have been knit together in their being thus caught up; hence they are related one to another in a bond which is essentially the bond of love, divine in the first instance and human as a consequence.

But the Church, like every grouping of humans, must exist in this world and must reflect, in some meaningful way, what is going on in this world. In other words, the Church is part of a created order which itself is dynamic, societal, and processive. In my view we can best understand that created order if we take seriously the insights which are found in the general philosophical conceptuality known as 'Process Thought.' Therefore I must say something about how that conceptuality looks at things. I shall do this under a few headings but very briefly—for further explanation the reader may wish to consult such books as my own *Lure of Divine Love* (Pilgrim Press and T. and T. Clark, 1981) or Peter N. Hamilton's *The Living God and the Modern World* (Hodder and Stoughton, 1968).

In the first place, as I have just said, ours is a world that is in process. That is to say, it is a changing or developing world—which does not imply automatic progress but which does stress the vital or living quality of its existence. Then, it is a world in which there are not 'things', or fixed and static substances, but 'becomings', events or occasions, which themselves are foci of energy and experience; only in a macroscopic sense is there such hardness, fixedness, and the like as appears to be the case to the naked eye. It is also a world which is inter-related, with everything influencing and affecting everything else—'no man', said John Donne, 'is an island entire unto itself', nor is anything else in the cosmos. If ours is a world of 'becoming', it is also a world of 'belonging.'

In such a world, there is a radical freedom, so that novelty may be chosen and may emerge in the creative advance. At the human level, this entails accountability for what is chosen in freedom. Nobody can escape this; and at other (and, as we usually say, 'lower') levels, there is an analogous freedom and accountability although of course not known consciously. Again, the world is such that in the long run, persuasion is more effective than coercion, even if this does not always seem to be so. And finally, God is related to the world so intimately and really that what has been said about the general principles required to describe the creation may be applied 'eminently' to deity. But this does not mean that God is not transcendent over the world. It means only that the creation reflects what is the basic character of God in the fulness of deity—the Creator is not denied by what goes on in creation, save when there is wilful wrongdoing. Or to put it in another way, the creation bears upon it what the ancient Fathers of the Church called *vestigia dei* —'traces or intimations of deity.'

Such a view of things does not deny for a moment the presence of evil in the creation nor the appalling reality of sinfulness in men and women. But it sees the entire created order as what might be called a great adventure in which God works ceaselessly to bring good out of evil, to make love triumphant over hatred and wrong, to establish truth over falsehood and error, and to express the divine beauty in that which is in the process of being created.

To my mind, this conceptuality is much closer to the general biblical interpretation than the more static philosophical systems which have so often been adopted by Christian theologians. But I shall not pursue this topic here; suffice it to say that in the present book it is assumed as a presupposition for the work of the preacher in proclaiming the gospel of God's active love in the Man Jesus and all that his appearance implies.

Now in a world like that, the Christian Church has its part and its place. It too is processive, as I have already urged; it is made up of living entities or human persons; it is a social affair, in which all its members influence and affect each other; it exists in freedom to decide what seems best in any given circumstance but must accept responsibility for what is decided and for the consequences of those decisions; and it lives and works in love —in the human loving which is both instrumental for and a reflection of the divine Love which in the event of Jesus Christ was (so Christians believe)—both enacted humanly in One of our own kind and also 'let loose' into the affairs of humanity in order to bring men and women to an ever more profound and enhancing existence in mutual sympathy, understanding, courageous defence of the right and good, and the promotion of rightness in all human relationships.

As such, the Church has its own identity. What is it that establishes identity in a world like the one I have been describing? Certainly it is not some substantial *thing* to which experiences happen. But if not that, then what is it that makes it a *this* rather than a *that?*

We can best arrive at an answer to this question by considering what in fact establishes the identity of any one of us. What is it that makes you *you* and me *me?* We are different one from another. Each of us is a human identity, specifically himself or herself. In an earlier day, people would talk about the 'soul' or would use some other similar term to indicate this identity. But nobody has been able to discover such a thing apart from the various experiences which are enjoyed. We *are* these experiences. That is, we are a routing of moments or occasions, taking place one after another; and these connected moments or occasions or experiences are what constitutes us for what we are. Where then is the identity?

I suggest that it is in the way in which each succeeding moment along that routing incorporates into itself what has taken place in the past, so that this past is not lost nor rejected but is felt or accepted ('prehended' is Whitehead's word for this) and incorporated into the next moment, along with whatever novelty or specific 'newness' that next moment includes. The past has what can be described as a causal efficacy upon the present. And there is an aim toward the future, so that each moment is already anticipatory of what will follow—that future has not yet happened, but the intimations of it are found in the way in which in the present it is being aimed for. So far so good. But at the human level there is a distinctive quality which we call awareness or self-consciousness, so that at each of the succeeding moments it is *I,* as somehow aware of that incorporated past, as existing in the present moment of decision and action, and as looking forward (with greater or less intensity) to what next will take place as the result of the choices made and the actions undertaken in the present.

All this may seem very abstract, at least in the fashion in which I have just put it. Nevertheless a little introspection will show it to be the way things go with us. What holds the whole routing together in a unity which has an enduring quality about it is my sense that it is precisely *I myself* who knows this past, exists in this present, and aims toward this future. In other words, it is my awareness of the past which has been efficacious in bringing me to the present and in providing the material (so to say) upon which by my several decisions (and the actions consequent upon them) a future is opened up for me to know and experience. This is my identity.

If we apply this sort of description to the Christian fellowship we may then say that it exists *from* its past, *in* its present, and *toward* its future. In that respect it is like any other social process of becoming and belonging. For I must not forget that this identity of mine is *with* others and *in* a world. Thus the Church is social in its character and is immersed in the affairs of the created order in which it has made its appearance. What is distinctive about it, about its identity, is the particular past which it inherits, what it does with that past, and how it works toward future goals. The past which the Christian community or tradition inherits is first of all the event from which it took its origin—Jesus Christ as an historical reality, with all that this includes such as the preparation in Judaism for his coming, the way in which he was received and understood in his own time, his own sense of vocation for whatever he undertook, and the way in which he has come to have significance for later generations. So it is that we may rightly say that the Church's identity is found in its existence 'in Christ' understood as 'important'— that is, as making a difference in the world—and as somehow focal in the relationship between God and that world, at least so far as we humans are concerned.

Since this is the case, the point now to be considered follows immediately. The Church exists, in its specific identity, to carry out a certain task; it has a function or functions which are also specifically its own. These are the affirmation or declaration of its originating event, the making of that event a contemporary reality through what we call worship, and the consequences of the event in producing a certain quality or mode of existence which (however various may be its manifestations) is recognizably in continuity with the originating event. In order to make all this possible, the Church also has a kind of succession in which the several functions are insistently undertaken and performed. In a profound sense, therefore, the Church's identity is indicated by those functions which are proper to its specific character.

To put this in traditional language, the Church manifests its Christian identity by proclaiming Jesus Christ, by making him available for men and women, by laboring to create and nourish a life in others which reflects and serves his purposes and his own quality of life. All of this in an historical succession in which the past of the tradition still lives in the present of contemporary human existence, with an aim toward fulfilment of the dominant and dominating purpose which in the earliest witness was declared as having been enacted in the originating event of Jesus Christ himself. So it is that the Church engages in preaching, worship, and the empowering of discipleship. The way in which these are done may differ from age to age, as would be inevitable in any social process which belongs in the world; but the several functions remain constant in themselves. They are what the Church *is for;* they characterize its very existence as the Church; and they are believed—here we come to the highly significant matter—to be the will and work of the God who was disclosed and whose power of love was released in what took place in Palestine two thousand years ago.

As I have just hinted, there are bound to be changes. In respect to proclamation, there will be different ways of presenting and interpreting the originating event as being important—in the most profound meaning of that word—and focal in the God-human relationship. There will be alterations in the fashion in which the worship, always essentially eucharistic and always an *anamnesis* (or the bringing of the originating event into the present) is undertaken. So also the manner in which life 'in Christ' will be wrought out will be different in succeeding ages. We are not asked to live archaically in first-century Palestine; neither are we supposed to engage in a mere repetition of formulae or actions or life such as were known and carried out at this or that particular moment in the past. In biblical language, the Spirit 'takes of the things of Christ and declares them unto us', always in a manner which is both appropriate to the Church's origin and also available for and intelligible in this or that given moment of the tradition's development. None the less, there is an identity and a continuity which is very real and very impressive.

In traditional Christian thought the Church has been defined as one, holy, catholic, and apostolic. Something needs to be said about each of these in the context of our discussion. I shall do this very briefly. First, the unity of the Church is in its abiding loyalty toward and its continuing reference to its Lord. This unity is not to be taken as demanding uniformity, since different people at different times and in different places will inevitably have their own way of expressing and realizing in concrete fact their common loyalty with its common reference to Jesus Christ. The outward manifestation of that basic unity has been lost, thanks to historical circumstances; but the reality of it remains —and one of the concerns of Christian people and their leaders must surely be to labor for its more obvious manifestation. A Church which is rent by divisions within itself is not a satisfactory expression of the oneness of Christian people with God in Christ and their oneness with each other in their communal existence.

As to holiness, this is of course to be seen as not so much a moral quality, although that is demanded, as in its 'belonging on God's side' and hence participant in the holiness which is God's own. The Christian fellowship is not identical with worldly affairs, however much it should be involved in those affairs if it is to fulfil its vocation. It cannot be separated from that world, to be sure; but precisely because of its nature and mission it must always be distinct from it. Otherwise, it will have nothing to give to the world but will become only a religious icing on the secular cake, providing religious approval to whatever the secular world may consider right and decent and respectable.

In its catholicity, the Church is for the whole world. It is catholic in the sense that it is (as I was brought up to say) 'for all people at all times and in all places.' There is more to its catholicity, however, than any such description can provide. The very word itself comes from the Greek phrase *kath'olou*, whose basic meaning is something like integrated, whole, harmonious. Thus the Church's catholicity, as our Eastern Orthodox brethren like to insist, is essentially its way of keeping together in an organic fashion its proclamation, worship, and life of witness, in continuity with its past, and with a due balance between and among all these. It is not a sectarian or 'clique-ish' society; it has about it a holistic quality which promotes and develops in its membership a similar wholeness of life, with belief, action, testimony, and loyalty knit together in an harmonious manner.

Apostolicity, like catholicity, has two senses. In the first place, as the word in its original Greek suggests, it is *sent:* the Church exists not only *for* a mission to the world but *as* a mission in the world. In that sense, holiness and apostolicity belong together. But in the second place, the Church's apostolicity tells us that it rests back upon and constantly witnesses to the first and originating moment of its existence. It does not reek of the contemporary, although it is bound to be concerned for that present moment of its life; it has a continuity which relates it inescapably to its earliest and originating days, on the one hand, and to the succeeding stages of its development as a living tradition, on the other hand.

All this finds its representation in the ministry of the fellowship. There is a ministry belonging to all Christian people as participant in the Body of Christ; as the Good Friday prayer puts it, 'every member of the same, in his vocation and ministry' is to serve the purposes of God in Christ. But without a specifically 'ordained' or authorized ministry, composed of persons who have been 'duly called, examined, and found qualified' to act for (but *not* instead of) that wider ministry of all Christian people, there would be lacking a sharp edge, a vivid and vital expression, of the more general mission and ministry. With this ordained ministry in its function of proclamation of the 'good news' or gospel of Jesus Christ this present book is concerned.

I must stress here what in the last paragraph was noted in a parenthesis: that the ordained ministry acts for and *not instead of* the ministry which belongs to each and every member of the fellowship. The difference between 'separate' and 'distinct' is to the point here. Ordained ministering is in no way separate from the wider ministry of Christian people; it is 'distinct' from that wider ministry, in that it functions for as it also represents the service which is proper to all who belong to the Church.

In past ages some have talked as if there were a gulf between these two; and in reaction from that utter separation, some have talked as if there were no distinction between them. The fact is that throughout Christian history, whatever may have been the theory accepted as valid, there has been precisely such a distinction. The way in which we can make sense of it is by seeing that the two are inseparably related but that inevitably (in a world like ours) there will be diversity: 'diversity of gifts but the same spirit.' I have just put the word spirit with a lower-case 's';

but I might quite as readily have put it with an upper-case 'S.' For the living reality of the Christian Church in which the Spirit of God—or the divine responsive movement to what was expressed in the event of Jesus Christ—is present and active is seen by the Christian ages to be not an accidental or merely historically-conditioned development. Rather, it is seen as in some very serious way guided and empowered by the Spirit of God released in Christ. Thus we can dare to say that the distinction between ordained and general ministry is not arbitrary or purely incidental; it is tied in with the operation of God as God purposes the Church to serve acceptably in this world of time and space.

In Christian teaching the Church is often spoken of as 'militant, expectant, and triumphant'—as the Church in this world of time and space, as the Church as it awaits final fulfilment, and as the Church 'in heaven.' Whatever we may think of this familiar description, one thing is apparent: the Christian fellowship, including all those who have been caught up into the love of God released in the event of Jesus Christ, is more than the visible community 'here on earth.' In some fashion, about which we can know nothing, those who have been 'soldiers and servants' of that same Christ in earlier ages and who have now died must not be forgotten but must be seen as participant in the life of God in a manner which is appropriate to that divine life. But if they are not forgotten by those who at present are living in the world, they most surely are not forgotten in God—God's memory is infallible and all-inclusive. Thus when we speak of death we are not talking about the finality of human existence. In God there is no *finis*, no ending, for Christian faith sees deity as everlasting.

With this in mind, preachers of the 'good news' needs always to remember that in their proclamation of that which in Christ God has 'determined, dared, and done' (in Christopher Smart's compelling words) they are speaking not just for the contemporary Church but for the whole body of faithful people. What is more, we cannot in our human ignorance and in our human finitude limit that body to those who have in some express fashion affirmed faith in Jesus Christ. God alone can know those who have responded, in whatever manner may have been possible for them in their time, place, and circumstances, to the divine self-disclosure. The Eastern Orthodox are prepared to include in the body of the Church in this extended sense the whole cosmos, even the natural order, quite as much as human existence on this planet. Here we are in the realm of speculation, of course, but we can say this at least: no preacher who knows his business and who is aware of 'the wideness of God's mercy' can dare to talk as if only those who have visibly and expressly professed Christian faith are the concern of a deity whose 'nature and name' is Love. Thus the preaching of the ordained minister must necessarily err, if it errs at all, on the side of generosity and charity. Who are we to attempt to narrow the divine compassion? In ways beyond our knowing, beyond our finding out, God cares for the whole creation.

What We Proclaim

THE TITLE of this chapter, although convenient, can also be misleading. For it is not so much *what* we proclaim as preachers; it is *whom* we proclaim. And the short answer to that question is that the ordained minister's function is to proclaim Jesus Christ and him crucified and risen from among the dead. To put it that way indicates the point of the entire Christian 'thing'; and it opens up for us the necessity for coming to understand, and then to declare to those who listen, the full significance of what God is up to in the whole world. For to say that Jesus Christ is *important*, as I have done again and again in the preceding chapter, is to say that he, as One who lived and worked at a given time and place, provides the clue to the divine nature and the divine activity wherever that may be found.

Although this is the case, the preaching of the gospel is not to be confused with theological discussion. Neither is it to be taken as discourse upon moral responsibility. In a later chapter we shall have occasion to point out that all preaching worthy of the name must be *theological,* by which I mean that it must be, as the very adjective indicates, 'a word about God' and hence about God's decisive action for humankind in the event we name when we say 'Jesus Christ.' But that is very different from saying that the sermon is to be about theology as a subject. Perhaps that is not a likely danger today. What is more probable is that preaching will be taken to be an exercise in moral exhortation. Again, however, we can say that while all preaching is to be *moral,* concerned to make clear the ethical implications of the gospel, it is not a matter of morality or ethics in itself. The distinction between preaching which has a moral quality and discussion of morality as such ought to be plain enough. Evelyn Underhill once said very wisely that the gospel is concerned with the *divine indicative*—'what God has done, is doing, and will do'—rather than with an *human imperative,* or what *we* should be doing, although the latter should be an inevitable consequence to the former.

Hence we may now turn to what the 'good news' is all about.

First of all, then, the gospel is not philosophical or religious speculation. Neither is it moral exhortation. I have already said that. It has to do with something that happened; it is about an event. To understand what this means, it is first necessary for us to see that the world is made up of events. In our opening chapter, we insisted upon this truth as part of a general conceptuality which makes sense in our time. Thus to talk about 'the *event* of Jesus Christ' is to talk about a reality that is not exceptional or unusual in the world—that is, so far as the 'event' aspect of it is concerned. But *this* event has the speciality which is proper to it; indeed, each and every occurrence in the creation has just such a quality of speciality—nobody is identical with anybody else; every happening in the world, especially as we come to what might be named 'the higher levels' in that world, is itself and nothing else. Hence it is entirely right to say that the event with which our Christian proclamation has to do is an event which is both particular and special.

When the preacher declares this event, he or she is saying something else too. That 'something else' is that the event of Jesus Christ is to be taken in faith as peculiarly and distinctively a disclosure of God, the dependable, worshipful, unsurpassable reality who is creatively at work in everything that takes place, even in that which is evil. This does not make God responsible for evil, for God never wills or wants anything that is against goodness, justice, truth, and beauty. Rather, it is simply the recognition that without the creative energy of God, providing aims, luring toward fulfilment of such aims, and always prepared to accept ~~creatively~~ *creaturely* achievement into the divine life, there would and could be no patterned creative order at all.

This fact tells us that whatever we may claim for Jesus Christ is not the denial of nor contradictory to the wider creative purpose and activity of deity. In the language of classical Christian theology, 'redemption' (as it is called) is another act of creation; it is in line with and part of the continuing divine working in the world. In other words, there is a general revelation of God in the world which provides the basic, indeed the cosmic, context for whatever may be said about the particular event with which we as Christians are concerned. God's general creative activity gives the setting for the particular activity of God in Jesus Christ.

But that activity in Christ *is* particular or special. Its significance is found in what as an event it brings about in the wider ongoing process. For as Whitehead insisted, an event or occurrence has its consequences—it brings into existence a 'stream of influence' which has affects in the world. What is thus distinctive about *this* event? I have already hinted at this when I spoke of its being a disclosure of God. While all occurrences disclose God in creative activity and doubtless also to some degree in redemptive activity in providing some guarantee of life's significance and value, this event is especially *important.* Its importance, or the fact that 'it matters' (again in Whiteheadian idiom), is for Christian faith found to be a vivid and focal revelation of what God is always and everywhere up to in the created order.

There is more than that, however. For the 'stream of influence' in this case has a specific quality about it. It is the releasing into the world of the divine power of love—and to this we must return in a few moments—which brings to those who are caught up into it a remarkable sense of 'comradeship and refreshment' —once again to use Whitehead's words—that both enables and ennobles human existence. Men and women who are participant in the continuing consequences of the event of Jesus Christ are given a new awareness of the divine perspective, the divine presentness in the world, and the power which makes human existence a rich and enriching experience. It is this double-quality—disclosure and release of God in the human creation— which explains why there is in Christian understanding an attempt to interpret or define *who* is the One about whom the proclamation is made.

What I have sought to do in the preceding paragraphs is to speak about what is usually styled 'incarnation' and 'atonement' but in an idiom which is appropriate both to the originating event and meaningful or intelligible to those who see the world in the way which I have described in our opening chapter. It may not be our idiom, this talk of 'incarnation' and 'atonement'; but the point is clear. Whatever terms may seem more suitable for us today, the reality that is affirmed remains the same. We are not to preach 'the Incarnation'; we are to preach Jesus Christ. We are not to preach 'the Atonement'; we are to preach Jesus Christ. Yet in each instance, that which the older language sought to express will be present in the preaching, since the event which is proclaimed *is* both disclosure of God in act and the source of the renewed life that is known within the Christian tradition as 'life in Christ.'

Now when we speak about an event, we are speaking about a fact that is somewhat complex. Any and every event at the human level has its antecedents, which have been efficacious in making that event possible. It has its specific location, so to say, in this or that particular time and place, centering in this or that particular person—what that person said and did; how that person was understood; what response was made to him and to his words and deeds. And a human event also has had results, since its decisions and consequent actions have made their particular contribution to the ongoing of things at the human level. Ralph Waldo Emerson spoke about this in a telling sentence; he said that 'Jesus Christ has been ploughed into history.' There can be no escaping him in that sense. Whether or not he has been recognized, he has brought about—or better, God has brought about through him—something that has made a difference.

That difference is not only in human affairs; it is also a difference in God, since God is always so related to the created order that what takes place in it has its influence and affect upon him or her, upon deity itself. While the divine character and nature do not change, the ways in which these are brought to bear upon the creation must change if God indeed is influenced and affected by what has taken place in the world. Simply phrased, God now has available for further divine activity in the human order the reality of what occurred in Jesus Christ.

Some readers may think that all this has been either meaningless talk or an unnecessary complication of basic Christian preaching. I do not think so; on the contrary, I believe that what has been said opens up for us, above all for the preacher of the gospel, valuable and fascinating ways of making sense of that gospel. Obviously enough the preacher will not speak in the fashion which I have adopted here. Yet he will have this background in his mind as he speaks Sunday by Sunday of the crucial importance of Jesus Christ.

Let us suppose that this preacher—call him Mr. Jones or Dr. Jones or Father Jones—enters the pulpit during a service of Christian worship. His task in that pulpit is to speak of Jesus Christ as the One to whom all that is going on that morning has a specific reference. He will seek to find appropriate ways to make the importance of that figure meaningful to the congregation. Perhaps he will take as the text for his sermon some incident in the gospels which tells of Jesus' doings or perhaps he will choose some bit of the teaching of Jesus as this is reported in the gospel narratives. He will not do what so often I have heard done by thoughtless ministers: simply repeat what the text says or attempt to elaborate on it as if it stood entirely by itself without context. No; he will endeavor to relate that given material (which has provided him with his starting-point) to two things. First, he will refer to the total picture of Jesus which the biblical record presents; in other words, he will use the specific act or teaching in context. And secondly, he will indicate how the total event, of which this act or teaching is a part, is both a disclosure of God and a reporting of its 'letting loose' in the world of the divine love-in-act.

An example may help to make my meaning clear. The incident which has been chosen for the morning sermon may be, shall we say, the story of Jesus and the Syro-Phoenician woman. She has come to ask Jesus to heal her daughter who is sick. The story relates how at first Jesus seems reluctant to do this; after all, he is a Jew in background and thought and she is a non-Jew who in the typical Jewish understanding of that time was considered 'a dog' before whom the treasures of Jewish conviction were not to be asserted. But the woman persists and finally Jesus consents to heal the daughter. Whatever may be said of its actual historical basis this story is a demonstration of the way in which the One who is being proclaimed learned through what as a human being he experienced. The tract to the Hebrews speaks of Jesus as having 'learned through what he suffered'; and the Greek verb in that text *means* 'experienced' rather than suffering in the more obvious English sense of the word. The preacher can now use the story to make plain to his hearers that the event of Jesus Christ is indeed on a genuinely human level; like all the rest of us, Jesus had to grow and develop in his awareness of the divine purpose in the world. He had to learn that it was not a purpose for Jews only; it was for the whole world.

But we must also see that in thus interpreting the given material as found in that narrative the preacher has a further task. Now he is to assert that what there was enacted is a veritable disclosure of God at work. God is not going to confine the divine revelation to any one section of humanity. The self-disclosure of God is for all people, wherever they may live and whatever may be their background or culture. At the same time, the preacher is to affirm that the release of the divine power of love, pointedly effectual in this particular incident in the reported healing of the daughter, is also for all people, bringing to them the 'comradeship and refreshment' of which they stand in need for the living of a truly human life.

Maybe this example will help to make my point clear. The apostolic Christian fellowship by whose interest and by whose memory this story came to be told—and here the contribution of form-critical and redaction study of the New Testament material is enormously helpful to us—did not use the incident as an interesting bit of historical information. It used the incident, as it used everything else that was given it in the oral tradition about Jesus which preceded the setting-down in written texts the story of Jesus, as a way in which the importance of the originating event was declared. Here, it said, the reality of the divine self-disclosure in act and the release of the divine love into human existence had a vivid and remarkable expression.

When a preacher understands this and is prepared to wrestle with it in his thinking before he does his actual preaching, he will have a deeper insight into the long-continuing Christian awareness of what God was 'up to' in the event of Jesus Christ and hence what God is always and everywhere 'up to' in the divine dealings with men and women in any and every culture.

What then does it come down to? The answer is that it comes

down to a conviction that God who is everywhere at work and everywhere available to men and women is indeed nothing other than Love-in-action. 'God is Love', says the first letter of St. John, summing up in that simple three-word phrase the conviction to which the primitive Christian community had come when it thought about, meditated upon, responded to, and in profound acceptance came to grasp what indeed God was 'up to' in that crucial event which took place at a given moment in history. The same writer, in the same chapter of his letter, goes on to say, 'Herein is love, not that we loved God'. He was realistic enough to see that any such statement is absurd on the face of it and is denied by the way humans fail in loving and hence are in desperate need of the assurance that love *is* central in things. 'Not that *we* loved God but that *he* loved us and sent his Son so that in him we might live.' As I once put it in another book, to us humans in our deep need, God comes with a loving deed—a deed which both discloses the divine nature and also makes available for men and women the possibility and power of responding to that divine activity in and as love.

There is a danger here. It is perfectly possible for a preacher simply to affirm that 'God is Love' as if it were an interesting significant speculation about the nature of the divine reality. The danger is that in doing this the preacher may suggest that this *is* but a human concept. However valuable and interesting that concept may be the preacher who knows his business cannot be content with any such bland statement. He must remember that precisely *because* God 'sent his Son' it is possible to affirm that God *is* indeed what in that event he enacted in human terms. In other words, preaching is never a nice piece of philosophical or religious thought. It is always proclamation—and as proclamation its focus is upon that which God does and not upon our human meditation on some supposed truth about God.

So far so good. Yet no preacher will wish to stop there. He will want to go on to draw out the practical implications of what he has proclaimed. He will feel bound to indicate at least some of the consequences which follow from acceptance of Jesus Christ, in the total integrity of the event of which he is the center, as a matter of Christian discipleship. It is at this point that the theological and moral aspects of Christian preaching become both relevant and inescapable. Let me say something briefly about these.

In the first place, so far as its theological aspect is concerned, we can see that those who respond in faith to Jesus Christ are impelled to read the whole of human existence, indeed the whole of their experience of the created world, in the light of that which has taken place in that important moment. They must be brought to see that here is the clue or key to the divine activity on all occasions, not just in this signal and decisive one. A man or woman who has been grasped by this central Christian conviction will thereafter be intent upon finding traces of the divine working in every aspect of his or her experience. In some fashion everything 'speaks of God as Love.' The world is the sphere or arena in which the divine Love is operative, recognized in various ways and with differing degrees of intensity. There is here a call to claim for God the whole world in its every aspect. To revert to the incident of the Syro-Phoenician woman and the response Jesus was led to make to her plea for help, we can now say that whenever and wherever there is healing in the world, it is the divine healing power which is behind such human endeavors as may be found desirable or necessary to effect that healing. At any time or place in which humankind is led to find value and significance in existence, it is the working of God which is present to provide the ground and explanation for such a realization. By extension every good deed, every struggle for justice and deliverance from oppression, every effort to care for and show concern about those who are in need, will be not merely a reflection of the divine mercy and righteousness but also an instrument for the bringing about of just such *shalom* or 'abundance of life' for God's human children. So one might go on, almost without ceasing, to show that response in faith to the action of God in *this* vivid moment has its implications and applications for the whole range of human life and experience.

In the second place, with respect to the moral aspect, there is a call for men and women, once they have been grasped by this central and transforming conviction, to labor on their part for exactly that establishment of loving relationships, with justice for all, with deliverance from oppression for those who are in bondage or undergoing deprivation and suffering, and for the establishment in the widest possible fashion of the *shalom* which is 'abundant life'—what Jesus is represented in the Fourth Gospel as saying was his vocation to bring to humans from his heavenly Father. The point is not that the preaching is to be a discussion of moral issues, such as might be entirely appropriate in a lecture or discussion-group; rather, the preaching is both a challenge to and a demand for a response which will represent in act that requirement of love in action in the world. Thus to present the moral implications is to do what Reinhold Niebuhr once said that all preaching ought to do: 'comfort the afflicted and afflict the comfortable.' No one who has really *heard* the gospel of God's righteous and holy love enacted and released in Jesus Christ can be content to 'sit at ease in Sion.' There is work to be done; and a consequence of genuine proclamation is the recognition that this is indeed the case.

Emil Brunner put this in a telling sentence: 'God's grace is a human task.' To accept and receive the loving-favor of God, which is what grace is all about, is at the same time to be impelled to act in a fashion which is appropriate to that response and acceptance. Otherwise the point of the gospel-message has been lost and those who think to respond in faith without response in act are deluding themselves and are forgetting other words put into the mouth of Jesus: 'By their fruits you will know them.' Jesus is also represented as having said that we are not to call him 'Lord, Lord' without doing that which his very lordship implies and expects. Thus it is clear that there is an inescapable moral aspect in all preaching, an aspect whose purpose is to awaken conscience and to move the hearers to do what Kierkegaard once styled 'the works of love.' Like the theological aspect, this moral side is inescapable; and a sermon which does not somehow require it is like 'salt that has lost its savor.'

I can think of no way more appropriate to close this chapter on the preaching of the gospel of Jesus Christ than by quoting some words by that remarkable English saint of the fourteenth century, Dame Julian of Norwich. In her account of her 'shewings', by which she meant the disclosures (or series of revelations) which she believed were given her in the cell which as an 'anchoress' or hermit she occupied adjoining St. Julian's Church in Norwich (hence the name which has been given her), she sets forth what she has learned to be the proper 'ghostly [spiritual] understanding' of the basic Christian message. She says that she heard God say to her, as she contemplated the Lord Jesus Christ, 'Would you learn your Lord's meaning? Learn it well: Love was his meaning. Who showed it to you? Love. What did he show to you? Love. Wherefore did he show it to you? Love. Hold yourself therein and you will learn more in the same. But you shall never know nor learn therein any other thing, without end.' Earlier in her book she says that she had seen 'a little thing, the quantity of a hazel nut, in the palm of [her] hand; and it was as round as a ball.' She had looked upon this with an 'eye of understanding and had thought: Whatever may this be? And it was answered generally thus: it is all that is made . . . it lasts, and ever shall, for that God loves it.'

Thus the beginning of all, as well as the end or purpose of all, is simply and plainly Love—Love-in-act, God as Love, God as the cosmic Lover whose sweep is all-inclusive but the application of which is particular for each and every man or woman or child. To proclaim that the historical event we name when we say Jesus Christ is important and decisive in our understanding of the God-human relationship is also to affirm—as the very heart of Christian faith and life—that it is, as Dante puts it at the end of *The Divine Comedy*, this unsurpassable Love which 'moves the sun and the other stars' and which seeks entrance into every human existence so that it may also move that existence toward loving. The end-result, as Dame Julian also wrote, is an awareness that 'God is nearer to us than our own soul; for God is the ground in whom our soul stands.' This awareness gives the assurance, again in Julian's words, that 'all shall be well, and all shall be well, and all manner of thing shall be well.'

The People to Whom We Preach

I N THE mid-1930s when I was first at the General Theological Seminary in New York, one of my colleagues and friends among the younger members of the faculty was Theodore Parker Ferris. He was academically brilliant and personally charming; what was more, as part-time assistant at Grace Church in downtown New York with duties confined to weekends, he showed himself a remarkable preacher. He preached at Evensong at Grace Church every third Sunday—and in those days Evensong was a service which was reasonably well-attended—and his sermons were so splendid that even now, after a half-century, I can remember some of them.

Later 'Ted' Ferris became rector of Emmanuel Church in Baltimore, Maryland, and then rector of Trinity Church in Boston, Massachusetts. He continued to be a magnificent preacher; most of the books which he published were simply his sermons slightly revised. I believe that he was the finest preacher I have ever heard. Alas, he died some fifteen years ago after a long and painful illness.

I have introduced him to the reader because in one of his essays, prepared for a volume of which I was an editor, he dealt with the task of preaching; and in that essay he used a phrase which is relevant to our present discussion. The job of a Christian preacher, he said, is to 'proclaim the given gospel to the given world.' The *given gospel*—that is to say, the gospel which has come to him from the Christian tradition which he represents and for which in his preaching function he speaks; *the given world*—that is to say, men and women in their actual concrete situation, with their interests and worries, their concerns and their problems. And the two are to go together, so that the gospel will be heard and (one hopes) accepted by those who hear its proclamation as directly relevant to their own lives.

We have already spoken about that gospel; this chapter will focus attention, as the title indicates, upon the people to whom we preach. But there is something else to be said and Ferris was a supreme representative of that 'something else.' He realized that in thus proclaiming the given gospel to the given world, it was necessary to find ways in which that proclamation could be brought home to men and women. Its manner of statement must be such that it would be intelligible to them and appropriate to their understanding of themselves and their world. It is at this point that another man comes to my mind. Leonard Hodgson had taught for a short time at the General Seminary, coming there from Magdalen College in Oxford where he had been Dean of Divinity; he returned to Oxford and for many years was Regius Professor in the Faculty of Divinity of that university. I knew him very well and am sure that he was one of the most alert and valuable members of the Oxford faculty during the 1930s and after the Second World War until his retirement.

Why does Hodgson come to my mind? Because those of us who were his students can never forget his insistence, made over and over again in various ways of phrasing, that precisely such an 'up-dating' of the significance of the Christian faith and its proclamation in preaching was not only desirable but essential. One of his ways of saying this has lately been made familiar by Dennis Nineham, now a professor at Bristol University but one-time Warden of Keble College in Oxford, who has quoted it again and again. It runs something like this: 'What must the truth be *for us*, if men and women who thought and spoke and wrote *like that* in their own day expressed its truth in the fashion in which they did in fact do this?' Here 'the truth' means both our way of understanding and stating the abiding faith of the Christian tradition *and* our way of affirming this in sermons.

To do this required, Hodgson made plain, that one must have a profound grasp of what in the past was taken to be the right way of seeing Christian faith and the gospel which is its grounding. Thus we are delivered from the merely contemporary and have entrance into all the richness of the historical tradition in which we stand. But at the same time parrot-like repetition of the older ways of speaking would not be right. It is our task in our time and place to discover how to re-affirm that abiding faith and its gospel grounding, so that what it is about, what it is concerned to assert, is brought home to men and women today.

In the preceding chapter I have sought to do just this. My own manner of doing it is by no means the only possible one; doubtless there can be and there are other and perhaps better ways of accomplishing the task. In any event, we need to bear in mind Whitehead's remarkable statement that 'Christ gave his life; it is for Christians to discern the doctrine.' Or to put it otherwise, the essential point is the event of Jesus Christ; all interpretations of its importance and all efforts to state its meaning will be the attempt to bring out both the essential elements in that event and also its significance for others. And it is precisely that which in the last chapter I have sought to do, in an idiom and context that to my mind is both appropriate to the originating witness and intelligible to contemporary people.

Now it will be useful for us to think about those people in their concrete situation and with their actual ways of looking at themselves and their world.

I have already given a sketch of the general world view which I believe is more or less assumed by thoughtful men and women today. It includes the processive, societal, dynamic picture of the cosmos; it sees that we have to do with events or happenings and not with inert and static 'things'; it insists on genuine freedom and readiness to accept the consequences of decisions made in that freedom; and it is prepared to see that however difficult this may seem to be, it is persuasion rather than coercion which in the long run is effective in the world. Doubtless very few people would phrase the matter in just those words; unquestionably most people are not able to work out such a world view in a consistent and coherent fashion. None the less, this *is* how they see things; and any proclamation of the gospel must be alert to that way of seeing things and must come to terms with its several emphases. But what about these men and women themselves? How do they see themselves, once they have got beneath superficial appearances and have been

brought to an awareness of their own existence, with its problems as well as its promise, its significance as well as whatever
calls that significance in question, with their hopes and their
fears?

The first thing to be said, to my mind, is that such people do
in fact feel that their existence has genuine significance—or
value, as we may prefer to phrase it. That existence matters to
them; they cannot accept the notion that they are meaningless
and accidental incidents in the cosmic enterprise. Of course
they may deny *in word* that their existence has such significance. But their actions contradict this denial and their attitude
toward themselves and others makes that contradiction apparent. Even the person who decides to commit suicide, because he
or she has been disappointed or frustrated or rejected, is really
asserting a sense of value, if only in the implicit assumption that
by ending life one can give it a meaning. The act of suicide is
a negative way of affirming a positive reality: 'At least I can do
this and thereby demonstrate, at least to myself, that I count
somehow in the scheme of things.'

But the very possibility of such an extreme act is a demonstration that along with a sense of life's significance there is a
feeling of discontent or dis-ease present in experience. Theodore Ferris said in one of his sermons that anybody who had
lived at all deeply must be conscious, usually in a dim and vague
manner, that he or she 'lives among broken things'—broken
hopes, broken dreams, broken ideals, broken relationships,
broken desires and aspirations; and that he or she is aware,
however dimly or vaguely, that all human existence, in each and
every instance of it, has about it just such a 'broken' quality.
Henry David Thoreau spoke of the 'quiet sense of desperation'
which now and again comes to all of us, perhaps when we are
unable to sleep at night or feel lonely and unaccepted. That deep
feeling is a token of the inescapable fact that our human existence, however rich or poor, prominent or obscure, successful or
unsuccessful we may be, is incomplete and needs fulfilment in
some fashion. This sort of feeling of human life is precisely what
St. Augustine was getting at when in a famous sentence in *The
Confessions* he said: 'Thou [God] has made us with a drive
towards thee; and our hearts are restless until they find their
rest in thee.'

One of the tasks of a preacher is to bring to those who hear him exactly this understanding of the human predicament: a genuine sense of value in human life but yet an accompanying grasp of its incompleteness, frustration, and inadequacy. The gospel of God in Christ speaks directly to that condition.

This does not imply that the more positive affirmation of life's importance is to be rejected. When Dietrich Bonhoeffer urged in his *Letters from Prison* that men and women have 'come of age', he was by no means saying that they were entirely mature, without any other interest than in their own accomplishments. He was asserting that they must be treated as those who have both responsibility and dignity and should be prepared to accept that fact. They no longer could 'run to Daddy' when things became difficult; neither could they be ready to shift the blame for their failures onto somebody else, certainly not onto whatever God there may be. They insisted that they were men and women who could at least try to act in a fashion appropriate to their having grown out of babyhood or childhood and advanced to late adolescence if not to full adulthood.

Thus people today are much concerned to assert, both in word and deed, that they can and do make decisions that count; that they do have a human dignity which is inalienable and which they must seek to awaken in their brothers and sisters; and that their responsibility is to do all that is in their power to make human existence a good and honest and true and harmonious one. This is why Bonhoeffer could also urge that it is a grievous mistake for a preacher of the Christian gospel to appeal to humans only in their weakness. The appeal must also be made to them in their strength, however that may be understood and implemented. He protested about the fashion in which those who proclaim the gospel often spend most of their time in stimulating an artificial sense of utter failure and sinfulness, so that then those preachers could declare that after all God still cares for such miserable wretches as he has induced his hearers to think themselves to be. Of course his attack was on a particular kind of Lutheran pietistic practice with which he was all too familiar. But what he said is equally relevant to other kinds of Christian proclamations and every preacher should bear in mind his almost bitter denunciation of this kind of approach.

To humans in their need God has come, and God still comes, with his unfailing love. But let us be sure that we grasp correctly what sort of love is of God and is God. There are moments when any man or woman likes to luxuriate in sentimentality and to indulge in a merely emotional feeling about life. Such sentimentality and emotionalism, however, has nothing to do with genuine love. It is the contradiction of human love; indeed, it is the exact opposite of divine love. The sort of love which enriches and ennobles human life has about it a quality of sternness and demand; it is adamant in wanting and expecting the best that is possible from the beloved. Divine love, likewise, is not easy and soft and undemanding; it has its adamant quality. Above all, genuine love is *passion.* It is passion in both senses of that word. First, it is strong and vigorous and can be represented (as in the Bible it *is* represented on numerous occasions) as much more like sexual passion than like sloppy acquiescence in whatever happens. And second, it is passion as suffering or anguish. The Spanish peasant saying that 'to make love is to declare one's sorrow' is very much to the point here. Human love requires such an identification with the one who is loved that his or her deepest and most painful experience is known and shared. Divine love as demonstrated in the event of Jesus Christ is a participation in the total existence of the creature, to the very limit of possibility. So St. John can say in the Fourth Gospel, that Jesus, 'having loved his own which were in the world, loved them *to the end'*—the Greek word for 'end' here is *telos* and that is to say 'unto the very limit', a limit which in Jesus was to the point of death for those whom he loved. God is not only *like* that. If indeed God was enacted in the human existence of Jesus, in a signal and decisive fashion, then God *is* that.

Rightly to proclaim the love of God is to declare that God's love is both accepting and demanding; both joyful and anguished; both fulfilment and judgment. And this speaks precisely to the human condition, as men and women understand that condition to be when they have been delivered from superficiality and triviality to an awareness of themselves as they really are.

The reader may have wondered why I have not yet said much about human sinfulness. After all, he or she may say, it is with this sinfulness that Christian preaching has to do. Only those

who are conscious of their sin, he or she may tell us, can really
hear the gospel. But as a matter of fact I *have* been talking of
sin, although not in conventional terms. Conventional terms
have little if any meaning to scores of our contempories; hence
they are better avoided. But the awareness of human inadequacy, human defection, human lack of potential fulfilment, and the
like is very much present in our fellow-humans. The preacher's
task is to show that this is what sinfulness is really about; and
then he or she is to go on to indicate that concrete actions,
words, or thoughts which are inhuman, negate right movement
toward fulfilment, and damage other persons and society. These
are the outward expression of just that deep lack of which they
are poignantly, if not always vividly, conscious. When Paul
Lehmann in an often quoted sentence said that 'God's purpose
for human life is to make it and keep it human' he was putting
the point in an admirable fashion—which helps to make contemporary people grasp both their high dignity as humans and
their defection from that possibility. At the same time he was
indicating very profoundly what God is 'up to' in the continual
coming to men and women which finds its climactic expression
in the event of Jesus Christ, so far as Christian understanding
is concerned, although we dare not be so exclusive or uncharitable as to rule out other ways for other people 'who know not the
Lord Jesus.'

If what has so far been said in this chapter comes anywhere
near the truth, it follows that preachers must acquaint themselves so far as they are able with the portrayal of the human
situation in novels, plays, poetry, as well as in the more techni-
cal and quasi-scientific writing of our time. But not only of *our*
time. For it is equally the case that the great inheritance in
literature which is available to us has its place here. While
today's conditions and circumstances differ in many respects
from those of earlier periods in our history, the basic situation
of and for humanity does not change greatly. Hence what has
been said by the Greek tragedians, by Vergil, by Dante, and by
many others, including such novelists as Dostoyevsky, Tur-
geniev, and others writers, as well as in the profound self-analy-
sis found in a Pascal or a Kierkegaard, needs to be given
attention. What Matthew Arnold styled 'the best that has been
thought and said' in the past has its contribution to make to the

preacher, if he or she is not to appear superficial or easy-going in presentation of the 'good news' of God's love-in-act as it meets human sensibility at its most profound.

The German-American thinker Paul Tillich, who died only a few years ago, believed that the Christian faith could only be rightly understood when it was recognized as providing the 'answer'—not of course in words or propositions but in the reality which is behind such statements—to the 'problems' which are posed by human existence as such. He was saying in his own idiom what I have been urging throughout this chapter. Another emphasis of Tillich's is relevant here when we are considering what 'it means to be human' and realize that our situation is such that the achievement of this human possibility is so frustrated and impeded. Tillich argued that basic in this respect is a deep feeling of what he called 'alienation and estrangement.' Humans are conscious of an estrangement from their right fulfilment and they sense an alienation or separation from their best selfhood, from other persons, from nature, and through all these from God who the source of their existence. In consequence, he said, they are not able to accept themselves as they are; nor can they accept others as *they* are. Humans are both unacceptable and unaccepting. The Christian gospel then comes to them with the assurance that they are accepted by a power greater than themselves; hence they are able to accept both themselves and others and to overcome their feeling of alienation and estrangement.

I believe that what Tillich was attempting to say in his own particular idiom (based as it was on a combination of existentialist analysis of human sensibility and the philosophical outlook found in German idealist thought) can be put in another fashion—and one which in my judgment speaks more directly to the ordinary man or woman. I have noticed that when in a sermon a reference is made to love, to the difficulty and pain of loving, to the necessity for us to know that we are loved, and the like, there is an immediate quickening of interest. The reason is obvious. Humans need love, which is to say that they need acceptance and sympathetic relationships in which there is both a giving and a receiving on each side. Often enough this need is spoken of in too easy a manner; it is sung about in sentimental songs and described in terms which can cheapen the reality which is at stake. Nevertheless it is a present fact; and even if we dislike the language that is popularly used, the truth is exactly as one popular song of the earlier part of this century put it: 'It's love and love alone the world is seeking.' To dismiss this is to fail to grasp something that is deepest and most real in human existence.

Our human difficulty, however, is that we are keenly aware that we are neither loved nor lovable; furthermore, we find it well-nigh impossible to 'live in love', as it is so often phrased. That is what is behind the sense of alienation and estrangement, along with the feeling of unacceptability, about which Tillich wrote. As a matter of fact, Tillich himself realized this. I happened to know him well; and in conversation or discussion, he was quite prepared to accept this way of speaking, although he personally preferred the rather more abstrict idiom which his background had suggested to him. Lack of love, failure in loving, inability gratefully to accept love toward oneself: here is another way of describing the defection of which men and women are conscious, even if they do not find it easy to put into words the awareness which is theirs.

The gospel which a preacher is to proclaim is to be seen as a bold affirmation, based upon the earliest Christian witness and the confirmation of that witness in the agelong Christian tradition, that we humans *are* loved, that we *can be* delivered from the lovelessness which makes us miserable and lonely, and that we *can be* enabled to return love even if very inadequately and partially. The love which is available for us is the Love which is God in action in the creation. It is the strong, vigorous, adamant yet gracious, loving which is the deepest need of humans and the final explanation of 'what makes the world go round'—to use the words of still another old popular song. When the day before yesterday the Beatles sang their lyric, 'You're nobody till somebody loves you', they were speaking to something which is felt most profoundly by men and women today as everyday.

This tells us, of course, that we are made—or better, that we humans are *being made,* for it is a continuing process—for each other and that nobody, in John Donne's already quoted famous phrase, 'is an island entire unto itself.' Doubtless there was a time when there was so strong an emphasis on 'rugged individu-

alism' that this social aspect of human existence tended to be
minimized and sometimes even forgotten. Doubtless too, in
reaction from that absurd pretence of individualistic independ-
ence, there has been a tendency to speak about our communal
existence as if to be a man or woman amounted only to being
an ant in an anthill, with little if any significant personal identity. Both these extremes must be avoided if we are to be realistic.
Furthermore, they must be avoided if we are to speak to the way
in which increasing numbers of people today understand their
humanity. We belong together, yet each of us counts in that
togetherness. To learn 'the lesson which Love us taught', as one
of Edmund Spenser's poems tells us, is to learn to accept our
human situation, to grasp our basic need, and to find an answer
to it in the affirmation that 'God so loved us that he gave
. . .'

An implication of this is that humans are not 'saved' merely
as individuals, all alone and by themselves; neither are they
'saved' when they are thought to be lost in the crowd', without
personal integrity such as they are sure must be theirs. The
people to whom we preach are those who are both personal and
social. Indeed the personality and the sociality belong together.
This is why the message of Love active in the world is a challenge to work so that in human ways and for human concerns
such loving may become the dominant quality of life. It is also
why the insistent human belief that justice for all people and
deliverance from oppression and servitude is met by the divine
Love that labors for precisely such justice and freedom. This is
no 'cold justice' and no impersonal interest in freedom for
others; it is a passionate caring which cannot be content unless
it is doing something; and that is a something which is social in
context yet also personal in its acceptance by each and every
son and daughter of God.

To talk of a 'personal gospel', as some have done, ought at the
same moment to be to talk of a 'social gospel.' For humans are
like that; and when they are most themselves they know this to
be true. Hence the preacher cannot rest content unless he or she
has spelled out the wider implications of God's loving act in the
event of Jesus Christ. This is why the moral side in preaching
cannot be neglected, although the preaching itself is not about

morality but about the activity of God which is the abiding basis
for moral concern.

The Setting in Worship

S O FAR we have spoken about the gospel which is to be
preached. It is the gospel of God's loving action in this
world, finding its focus for us in what took place in Palestine in the life of Jesus Christ as this was acted out and met
response. We have also spoken of the people to whom that
gospel is to be preached. These people are men and women and
children who among the 'sundry and manifold changes of this
world' need desperately to be given the assurance that in and
behind and through all created things there is a divine Love, a
cosmic Lover, who provides a grounding for their dim sense that
human life has an abiding value or significance which nothing
can destroy.

But the proper setting for that proclamation to such people is
normally in the setting of Christian worship. Worship is the
human activity in which the divine Love is acknowledged, accepted, and gladly received. When Christian people obey the
admonition in the New Testament tractate called *Hebrews* that
they are 'not to forsake the gathering of themselves together',
they come to engage in a corporate act or 'liturgy.' Thus to join
oneself with others who hold the faith—sometimes with utmost
seriousness, sometimes and often with little more than the
desire to do exactly this—is to express in a visible way the
sense of companionship or human fellowship which is not only
a natural desire but is also and supremely an outward sign of
their intentional discipleship.

Other religious traditions, generally speaking, with the exception of the Jewish faith which is the background of specifically Christian faith, do not seem to have this necessity of corporate worship as part of their very existence. Such worship, in company with brothers and sisters in the faith, is no incidental part of the total Christian way of life; rather, it is integral to it and essential for it. Nor does it depend upon emotional conditions; for the Christian ages it has been both a privilege and a *duty.* Thus it is altogether right that the preaching of the gospel or 'good news' should have for its fitting setting precisely these occasions of corporate worship.

It was Martin Luther, the great Reformer in Germany, who wrote about the way in which the sacrament of the Lord's Supper was a means for receiving into one's life the reality of 'the Word' preached in the sermon which he wished always to be associated with the sacramental celebration. The two held together as a single action were to be the main Sunday service of worship for every Christian. So also the Swiss Reformer John Calvin wanted to have the regular Sunday service in Geneva a combination of Eucharist and sermon. The English Reformers, in the Prayer Book which was prepared by Thomas Cranmer in 1549, had exactly the same intention—as is shown by their providing that only at the eucharistic celebration was there to be the collection of alms and the making of parochial announcements.

Failure to follow the wishes of these Reformers, which was of course identical with the ancient practice of the Church, has been a tragedy. The reasons for this failure are probably to a large degree 'social', in that laypeople were not sufficiently instructed to see the point, while working conditions doubtless also made their contribution. Another reason, as we can see in Scotland, has been the fear that by too frequent observance of the sacrament there would be a cheapening of the rite and forgetfulness of its importance. But whatever may have been the reason, the fact remains that it is only in our own time that the Reformed churches have begun to recover the centrality of the Eucharist in worship, while in England (and elsewhere in the Anglican Communion) the Tractarian movement and its Anglo-Catholic successor was responsible for the recovery of the traditional observance of the Lord's Day. In Roman Catholic circles, of course, the Eucharist or Mass has always been the chief service, but unfortunately (until Vatican II required a sermon or homily at every major celebration of the sacrament) the preaching of the gospel has not always or often been associated with the rite. Fortunately this defect has now been remedied; and there is a growing agreement among all Christian people that the two—sacrament and sermon—belong together and that every Christian ought to be present and assist at such an act of worship every Sunday.

I have said all this because I wish to emphasize in this chapter that the proper setting for preaching should be the Eucharist—although of course there will be other important occasions when the proclamation of the gospel will stand by itself or take place in other contexts. Evangelistic meetings, evening non-sacramental worship, outdoor preaching (as in London at the Tower and in Hyde Park), and similar times and places may very well include an address whose main purpose will be the presentation of the reality of Jesus Christ to those who otherwise would not know about him. But as I have said, historically the normative occasion for preaching is in connection with the Eucharist. It will be proper, therefore, to discuss in this chapter the way in which that sacramental action is indeed, as Luther said, the setting-forth of the Gospel which is presupposed whenever the Eucharist is celebrated.

There is a remarkable parallel between the Eucharist as an action in which the Christian fellowship regularly engages and the meaning of preaching as it proclaims the event of Jesus Christ, what that event has accomplished, and what its 'benefits', or results in the life of the believer, bring to the believer.

First of all, then, let me stress that the Eucharist is indeed an action. The gospel narratives tell us that at the Last Supper Jesus said that his disciples were to *do* this 'in remembrance' of him. They were not told to think about him or meditate on his self-sacrifice on Calvary. They were to *do* something; and this, which they were told to do, has in fact been done regularly and faithfully throughout the history of the Christian community. As Dom Gregory Dix, in a now famous section of his book *The Shape of the Liturgy,* put the matter, Christians through the ages have known of no better and more appropriate way to 'remember' Jesus than by participating in the offering of the Eucharist as 'the continual memory' of his passion and death—which also means, of course, the life which preceded Calvary and the knowledge of the risen Lord which followed the crucifixion. Here are Dix's splendid words: 'Jesus told his friends to do this, and they have done it always since. Was ever another command so obeyed? For century after century, spreading slowly to every continent and country and among every race on earth, this action has been done, in every conceivable human circumstance, for every conceivable human need from infancy and before it to extreme old age and after it, from the pinnacles of earthly greatness to the refuge of fugitives in the caves and dens of the earth. Men have found no better thing than this to do for kings at their crowning and for criminals going to the scaffold; for armies in triumph or for a bride and bridegroom in a little country church; for the wisdom of a Parliament or for a sick old woman afraid to die ... One could fill many pages with the reasons why men have done this, and not tell a hundredth part of them. And best of all, week by week and month by month, on a hundred thousand successive Sundays, faithfully, unfailingly, across all the parishes of Christendom, the pastors have done this just to make the *plebs sancta dei*—the holy common people of God.'

In recent years, all Christian groups have recovered an awareness of the way in which that memory includes, indeed *is,* the whole action in its integrity. It is not only in the specific 'words of institution' that this occurs; the presentness of the Lord is accomplished through the entire rite as something that is *done,* not merely thought about gratefully and devoutly.

Something done: the Eucharist is in itself an event; it can be properly understood and adequately interpreted only in the light of that fact. But as I have just said, it is an event which has a remarkable parallel to the originating Christian event of Jesus Christ; and this is one reason why it is appropriately the setting for the proclamation or preaching of the Lord who is central to the historical moment.

Let us first indicate the elements or aspects of the eucharistic event. Then we shall be enabled to trace out what I have called the parallel which exists between the two events, one historical and in the past, the other contemporary and very much in the present. Nor is that parallel nothing more than an interesting

accident; I believe that it is a parallel so profound and so reveal-
ing that it gives us insight into the nature of the Eucharist as the
chief piece of Christian worship while it also provides us with
the clue as to how the gospel which is proclaimed can become
the life-giving reality of the Christian tradition down the ages to
the present day.

The elements or aspects to which I now direct attention must
be discussed in some detail, but only a book or a series of books
could do justice to their significance. In the space at our dispos-
al, however, we may yet say enough to point toward their indispensable expression of our responding Christian faith as it is
confronted by the action of God in Jesus Christ 'for us men and
for our salvation.'

First, the action of the Eucharist is a memorial. The sense in
which this is true must be explored; it will suffice at the moment
if we repeat once again that 'memorial' here does not indicate
mental reverie but rather a genuine and vital *re-call* of the past
into the immediacy of present experience. Secondly, as an action the Eucharist is sacrificial in quality, since it has to do with
an oblation, offering, or self-giving which was the characteristic
mark of the life of Jesus in obedience to what he took to be the
vocation given him by his heavenly Father. Thirdly, the eucharistic action has to do with a making-present, or as I prefer to
put it 'a presentness', of the originating Christian event, brought
into the 'here and now' of contemporary Christian existence.
Fourthly, the Eucharist as action establishes, thanks to that
'presentness', a communion between God and humanity and
also among those men and women who are privileged to assist
at the celebration of the sacrament. Fifthly, the Eucharist as
action is given an imperative quality in that it results in a 'sending out' or a mission received by the worshipers, which they are
to carry on in their daily life of witness and work in the world
of human affairs.

With these five there is an overarching and inclusive renewal
of the kind of human existence which we have seen that St. Paul
could define as 'life in Christ', with all that this implies for the
Apostle and with all that it still implies for the Christian believer
today.

Perhaps it is already evident how these aspects and elements
which are thus characteristic of eucharistic observance have

their correspondence to the proclamation of the gospel. For that proclamation is concerned to affirm that the Jesus Christ who is so central to it is no mere figure of the past; he is remembered in the most serious sense as still making a difference. Again, when he is proclaimed, he is proclaimed in the full integrity of his human life which from beginning to end, as the apostolic witness indicates, was an obedience in self-giving in response to the vocation given him by God. It is also an insistence that in thus remembering the totality of his life, there is established a present awareness of him as active in the world today through the Spirit was released in and through him. There is the bold affirmation that through the event of which he is the center a relationship between God and humankind, and among men and women too, has been made possible, with its own distinctive quality. And proclamation leads to mission, since those who have genuinely heard the preaching are impelled to act upon it in such a way that in what they say, think, and do there is a witness to which testimony is given and a task to which they are called. Finally, because of all this, the Christian proclamation has as its end-product the bringing to the hearers an awareness of the reality of newness of life—what in the Fourth Gospel is called 'eternal life' and 'abundant life', what St. Paul is getting at when he speaks of 'life in Christ' as possessing a particular and specific quality of giving-and-receiving in love, in divine Love which is then reflected and enacted in human loving, with its association with justice and righteousness and deliverance from loveless existence.

We have already said a great deal about 'memory'; here I wish only to remark that the use of the Process conceptuality can be of great help to us here. That conceptuality puts an emphasis upon the way in which past events have their efficacy in the present and prepare for the future. While in one sense they 'perish', to use Whitehead's word, in another and more profound sense they are never lost because they are, so to say, 'immanent' in what follows them and upon which they have had their enormous influence. They provide the material which is 'prehended' or grasped in the present. So it is that in the eucharistic memorial there is a genuine bringing of the event which is thus 'remembered' into the immediacy of the new moment in which the celebration takes place. There is a similarity here to the Jewish observance of the Passover *seder*. In that supper, shared by a Jewish family once a year, the deliverance of the Jewish people from the Egyptians, as recounted in the book Exodus in the Old Testament, is the central point of the occasion. When the father of the family recounts the story of that deliverance, it is no mere mental recollection which is in view; rather, it is the making into a contemporary event, in which those present are able to share, of that which (in Jewish belief) God accomplished at the Red Sea many centuries ago. The eucharistic memorial is similarly a bringing of what might have been 'the dead past' into the present moment. The negro spiritual asks, 'Were you there when they crucified my Lord?' To this the Christian answer is 'Yes, I *am* there whenever the command of Jesus to "do this" is obeyed by those who are of the Christian fellowship.' Furthermore, we may point out that Rudolph Bultmann, the distinguished German form-critic, was accustomed to urge that whenever the gospel was faithfully preached there was also a bringing of the past event of the crucifixion into the immediacy of the present. Thus for him the preaching was, so to say, an occasion of 'resurrection', since the Lord who died on Calvary was now available and actively expressed as he was proclaimed.

But this brings us to the second element, sacrifice. For as in the preaching, so also in the celebration, the self-offering of Jesus as known as the Lord's action at the Last Supper is remembered. We have seen that in Christian understanding the death of Jesus is always to be set in the context of his total existence in self-dedication to God in fulfilling the vocation which he believed had been given him. In this sense, as we can see, there is deep truth in the medieval saying *tota vita Christi misterium crucis*—'the entire life of Christ is the mystery of the Cross'— because, as the apostolic witness testifies, Jesus gave himself at all times and in all places and with all those who met him, as One obedient to the divine Father's purpose for him. Thus the notion of eucharistic sacrifice is not confined to the specific point of actual death; it includes the whole of the event of which Jesus is the center. All that went before Calvary was preparation for or (better) was anticipation of the death. What followed afterward, in the conviction that the Lord who had died was the Lord who was raised by God from 'among the dead', is equally a part of the picture. The preaching declares this to be the case; the celebration enacts it in a visible and available manner.

In doing this, the memorial is the way in which what I have styled the presentness of the Lord is made possible. Jesus is not taken to be only the One who walked and taught and acted in Palestine two thousand years ago. He is the One who even now, through the operation of the Holy Spirit whose work (as I was taught in my childhood) is 'to make Jesus present still', is known to and available for his people. In the Process conceptuality this is given a context which can be most helpful to us. That conceptuality speaks of the fashion in which events or occasions are received into the divine life, making a difference to God; it also speaks of the way in which God gives back, as it were, the past event—it 'floods back into the world', in Whitehead's way of saying it—so that it is not 'dead and gone' but is effectual in the ongoing relationship between God and the world. Thus the risen Lord, which is to say the Jesus who now is incorporated into the divine reality as an everlasting element in that reality, is made a present fact in the existence of those who will respond to him and obey his will, to serve as he did for the increase of 'amorization' in the world. Here once more the preaching and the celebration are concerned to accomplish the same thing.

Through that renewed presentness there is opened up a communion between God, defined in Christ, and the world of human life. At the same time, and as a necessary consequence, there is a communion among those who have been caught up into Christ, so that when the Eucharist takes place those who are assisting at its observance find themselves belonging with each other in a new and vitalizing fashion. This is not simply another instance of human friendship and companionship, because now it is so rooted and grounded in the divine accomplishment that it has about it an enduring quality which nothing can destroy. It is 'the communion of saints', in which those 'saints' (which in New Testament usage indicates all 'faithful people') are given a unity which is made possible because they have become 'sharers in the divine nature.' So the Petrine epistle puts it; and this does not mean any identification of divinity and humanity, as if 'man became God', but rather means such profound participation in God's life, available in what God has done in Christ, that while their oneness is indeed on the level of human existence it is also and more significantly 'in the heavenlies' where men and women 'seek that which is above' their ordinary human aims and are enabled to know something of the divine reality as the dominant principle of their continuing existence. The preaching of the gospel has precisely the same purpose: the bringing of men and women into an abiding communion with deity and with one another, here and always. And it is worth saying once more that this life together is nothing other than 'life in love', human love because also sharing in divine Love, in God who *is* Love-in-act.

Finally there is the mission, or the sending', which is integral to the sacramental rite. In the old Roman Catholic liturgy of the Mass the words of dismissal at the end were *'Ite, missa est.'* Sometimes this phrase has been translated simply as 'You are now to leave because the Mass is finished.' But that translation is inadequate. The Latin verb *mittere*, of which 'missa' is a participial form, has a much deeper sense; it is a way of saying that 'you are now sent out . . .' *Sent out* or given a mission, then, for doing the 'works of Love' in the world. The prayer of thanksgiving in both Latin and English liturgies today makes this abundantly clear. And this is exactly what responsible preaching also has in view. When the proclamation of the 'good news' has ended, there is no conclusion of the matter; in a very serious sense the proclamation continues to be effectual as both requiring and empowering a life that is 'in Christ' and hence a life in which the believer is to express in all that he or she says or does the reality of the divine Love in which that person is now a participant. So it is that the last of the points made some pages back, summing up the several elements of eucharistic action, comes to the fore. The point of the whole exercise, as also the point of the preaching of the gospel, is the establishment of the specifically Christ-existence, in which the 'love of God in Christ Jesus our Lord' is known, shared, enacted, and manifested.

I have said that the proclamation of the gospel and the celebration of the sacrament constitute together the normative worship of the Christian community. Yet even when that is not realized in concrete fact there is always in Christian worship of any kind a similar pattern.

In conservative evangelical circles, whether in the Anglican Communion or in churches of a 'reformed' type, the recovery of this normative worship in eucharistic observance has not always been achieved, although there are many signs which point toward a growing awareness of its importance and centrality. But it is still true that when the chief act of worship on a Sunday is in Anglican circles Mattins or Morning Prayer and in 'reformed' churches a much more sermon-centered type of worship, there is also a liturgical or quasi-liturgical setting for the proclamation of the gospel. The hymns, readings, and prayers are directed toward a genuine awakening, among those who are present, of the 'memory' (in the deep sense I have indicated) of the originating event, with its insistence on the full obedience of Jesus in his self-offering to the Father on behalf of his human brothers and sisters. There is an awareness of his presentness and hence a renewed sense of communion with God in Christ and with one another; there is an imperative for Christian witness and work; and there is a seeking of a life which is 'in Christ' and which reflects and enacts his own loving concern for others. It would be unfair, as well as uncharitable, to exclude such worship from the tradition which in more 'catholic' circles finds its expression in Eucharist-proclamation worship.

As I have urged before, there can also be preaching which is not in the context of worship at all. This may be necessary when the more traditional context would make little if any sense to those who must be reached. None the less, there is much truth in the saying that if we wish to tell the non-Christian what the Christian enterprise is about, the best thing that we can do is to persuade that person to attend a Sunday celebration of the Eucharist in which there is also and of necessity a proclamation of Christ. Obviously this cannot always, perhaps often, be done, since for a great many people today the whole idea of worship has little meaning. Nor are the services of worship readily intelligible to somebody who has no acquaintance with the tradition of which it is an expression. Here there is a very special responsibility laid on those who do share the tradition, above all on those whose task it is to prepare the forms of worship which are used regularly in the churches.

As everyone knows, ours is a time when there has been much liturgical revision and in which new services have been prepared for use in the parishes. This is certainly to be welcomed, since frequently the idiom which is conventional in Christian circles is very difficult for contemporary people to understand. I believe, however, that a good deal of this revision has been misguided or ill-informed. I shall end this chapter with a few comments which may be relevant here.

First of all, responsible liturgical revision cannot consist only in the use of more contemporary language or in the avoidance of what are known as 'sexist' phrases (which are so dominantly masculine that women often feel excluded from what is going on) or in a return to biblical idiom to replace other (perhaps medieval) terminology. We shall be seeing in a later chapter that the biblical idiom is not to be taken in the wooden fashion which so often such revisions seem to follow. It is also true that merely putting 'You' where more traditionally 'Thou' would have been used in address to deity is hardly sufficient. Again, entirely contemporary language can so much 'reek of the present moment' that the sense of belonging to an agelong tradition can be lost or seriously diminished. These are valid criticisms of a good deal that has been done by the liturgical commissions set up by Christian communions.

I myself have 'no wisdom', as the saying goes, which will provide appropriate guidelines for these commissions. But it seems to me that if the preaching of the gospel is today to be undertaken in an idiom, and with the use of materials, that speak directly and meaningfully to men and women of our own time, so also the services of worship, above all the Eucharist, must also be carried on in just that same way, with direct and meaningful conveyance of the insights and understanding of Christian faith, so that the service of worship will not seem archaic, even archaeological, in nature, and lacking reference to or relevance for those who by necessity live in a world that is interpreted differently from the way in which it was interpreted in an earlier age. To accomplish this liturgically is no easy matter, any more than is the finding of language for the authentic proclamation of the authentic gospel. The best that can be hoped for is that experts do the job to the best of their ability in the expectation that others may correct and amend what has been proposed. For my own part, I believe that most of the revisions which have now been adopted are along the right lines; what they require is such modification here and there as shall meet responsible criticism.

In any event, what is said, like what is done, in the worship of the Church must be sufficiently in line with the inherited usage that it is recognizably Christian in its historical emphasis, while at the same time it is sufficiently intelligible to contemporary experience and understanding. To put it in the way in which others have spoken, both eucharistic celebration and proclamation of the gospel should always be in a fashion that is appropriate to the witness of the Christian past *and at the same time* available for the thinking and feeling of the people who take part. Otherwise we shall be either disloyal to our own Christian past or absurdly anachronistic.

The Preacher

BOTH AS the title for this chapter and frequently in the course of our discussion I have used the word 'preacher.' My reason for doing so is obvious; the topic which we are considering is the proclamation of the gospel which in common parlance is called 'preaching'; and hence the person to whom has been entrusted this task as part of his responsibility as an ordained minister is frequently called 'preacher.' As a matter of fact, there are also Christian groups in which that is the normal term for an ordained person.

It is important, however, to stress that in the wider Christian tradition preaching is but one of the functions of those who have been ordained. In the Catholic tradition an ordained person is commonly known as a priest; in the Reformed communions he or she is called an elder or presbyter; in all Christian thought he or she has been known as a minister, with duties that are distinctively his or hers through having been 'set apart' to act representatively for the wider ministry of all Christian people. That is the appropriate context for whatever we may wish to say about the duty of preaching or the proclamation of the 'good news.' This fact is important not only in respect to 'church order' but also in very practical ways.

I say this because I am convinced that the preaching of the gospel is best done by one who has a more extended range of ministerial obligations. Some have talked about the 'ministry of prophecy', which is indeed a very real aspect of the Church's work. But prophets are not ordained; they are called by God, usually from among the laity, to speak a word in season. In the Old Testament this is plain enough; only Isaiah among the canonical prophets whose oracles are reported to us was a member of the Jewish priesthood. In the history of the Christian Church prophets have appeared from time to time, sometimes of course from the ordained ministry but more frequently without the benefit of such authorization to act on behalf of the community. This is why I for one object to the kind of discussion which presumes that the preaching function is in itself a prophetic one. There is an important distinction here which must not be forgotten.

Many do not like the word 'priest' as a term to describe the ordained person; but it is a relatively harmless usage! After all, as a well-known saying in England centuries ago put it, 'new priest is but old presbyter.' Which is to say, the leader of the community in this or that place acts as the designated 'elder' and performs what can rightly be known as priestly functions, even if that particular word is not employed. The job of the ordained person, acting always on behalf of the Church itself and always as an 'under-shepherd' of the Good Shepherd who is Christ, is to labor as one who seeks to bring God to God's human children and to bring those human children to God. It is, so to say, a mediatorial task, although as such it is not one's own by any gift or quality which he or she may think to be personal to the minister; it is by designation to serve representatively for the mediatorship which Christian faith assigns to the Lord alone in any ultimate and abiding sense.

But the very term 'under-shepherd' which I have just used will be helpful to us. A shepherd is a 'pastor'; and basic to all ministering by those ordained is this sort of service. To use the perhaps outmoded idiom of an earlier day, the ordained person is to care for the flock of Christ, to see that they are fed and tended, to aid them and urge them to be what they are—Christ's people gathered into a community whose chief Shepherd is the Lord but on whose behalf the ordained person is to do a particular sort of work. Thus we might say that preaching is part of a pastoral ministry; it is a way, if not the chief nor the only way, in which the care of the people of God is to be carried out. If with this we associate the usual 'catholic' view that a priest is especially assigned the responsibility of administering the sacraments of the Church and in particular the celebration of the Eucharist, we have a proper setting or context for the labor of proclamation. There is a balance here, a proportionate arrangement of duties and obligations.

Having said this, as a way of putting the matter in the right perspective, we may now go on to consider some necessary aspects of the preacher's own existence which provide the background for the duties to be carried out in preaching. I shall mention several which seem to me to be inescapable for any responsible minister.

The first thing that should be said is that a responsible preacher is not concerned to proclaim his or her own opinions, ideas, or beliefs. Because a preacher is representing the agelong Christian tradition, what he or she is expected to do is to speak forcibly and boldly on behalf of that tradition. This is not to say that a preacher will be a parrot who repeats over and over again either the exact words learned in theological school or assumes that the 'everlasting gospel' does not stand in need of continual 'up-dating.' The essence of the proclamation is the importance of the event of Jesus Christ as the disclosure of the divine reality at work everywhere in the world and the releasing of the divine love which brings *shalom* to the sons and daughters of the human race. Obviously every preacher will have his or her own way of making the proclamation; his or her own understanding of it, as well as his or her own experience of what it entails, which will inevitably affect the way in which he or she must speak. At the same time, there is some truth in the remark made by a very young clergyman who when rebuked by a lady in his congregation because he was such a young man that he had no business speaking so forcibly to his congregation replied, 'Madam, when I put a stole around my shoulders I am two thousand years old!' Of course that was both a silly and a presumptuous remark. But as I have said, it has its truth, which is simply that the preacher, representing the historic Christian tradition, is commissioned to proclaim the *Church's* gospel, by which it lives and for whose declaration it has been given the inescapable responsibility. This need not, for a moment, suggest there will be nothing fresh and new in the preaching; after all, the gospel is both ever-old and ever-new, which means that it is about a given affirmation which is to be adapted to (but not altered for) the people to whom it is being brought.

To say that, of course, is also to say that a preacher needs to be an informed person. The years which such an one spends in study preparing for the exercise of ministry is intended to make him or her such an informed person. I remember a young priest whom I knew who told me with some pride that he had not 'cracked a theological book' (as he phrased it) since he had left theological college. I could only think that his preaching must be pretty inadequate; and when the next day I heard his sermon I found that I had thought correctly. It was nothing but a series of outworn clichés, showing that he had failed entirely to keep himself alert to new ways in which the old truth may be said; while he also made the sad mistake of assuming that whatever seemed to him interesting or significant constituted in itself the gospel which he had been ordained to preach. I did not want him to preach theology; as I have said, that would not be genuine preaching at all. But I did wish that he had kept himself sufficiently informed so that when and as and if he did (almost by accident!) preach that gospel it would not appear to be either his own invention or (even worse) so stale and pointless that nobody could be expected to take it seriously.

Again, a preacher who knows his or her business will be aware of the people to whom the sermon is addressed. I have spoken about this in an earlier chapter; here I need only say that one of the great assets of the pastor-preacher is precisely that acquaintance with the men and women who assist at worship will provide real awareness of how those people stand in need of what is proclaimed and how they may best be helped to assimilate the reality which in Christian faith is given to the world. I may speak personally here, but with due apology for doing so. Most of my preaching in recent years has been in a college chapel at services which are attended by hundreds of people about whom I know little if anything. I find it extremely difficult to put myself in their place and to try so to preach that the content of my sermon—which is always, so far as I can make it, the proclamation of the importance of the event of Jesus Christ as decisive and focal in the God-human relationship— can be brought home to my auditors. Fortunately, in addition to preaching at these great and crowded services in our chapel I have had the opportunity quite regularly to preach briefly to the young men and young women of the college who have come on Sunday evenings to what we call 'college communion.' I *know* them, often very well; and I find that I can speak to them with confidence and the sense of meeting to some degree their needs and speaking to 'their condition', as Quakers would put it. This means that there is what might be called a much more personal relationship between us, which is almost entirely lacking on the other occasions to which I have referred.

In another piece of writing I have told about a clergyman whom I knew slightly during my years of teaching in New York City. This older man, I learned, had a practice which seems to me admirable but which so far as I know is very seldom found. A day or two before he was to preach at the main Sunday Eucharist he would go into the church which he had served for many years. There he would seat himself at various places, front and back and in the middle, calling to mind the persons, young and old, who normally occupied those places at the service. As a faithful and devoted pastor he was well-acquainted with them all. He would ask himself, in each place, 'What does John or Mary or Samuel or Helen need to have said to them, so that they may more truly and deeply understand and experience the meaning for each of them of that which God has accomplished in Jesus Christ?' Then in the preparation of the sermon he was to preach on the Sunday, he would do this with them in mind, so that he might be able to some degree at least to make the gospel relevant to them and meaningful for them, precisely in their given situation and need. I was told that this priest was not only much loved by his people but was considered by them to be a highly effective preacher. No wonder!

Another matter which needs stressing is that a preacher like any Christian needs to keep his or her own faith fresh and alive. This is easy enough to say but its implementation requires a life of Christian discipleship which is nourished by prayer and meditation. In other words, such a preacher should be devout in the best sense of that word. I have spoken of my old friend Theodore Ferris. He once told me that he not only spent many hours working on what as delivered seemed very simple and straightforward both in expression and in content. He also brought his preparation and the sermon which was its result

into his own praying. He did not expect that God would give him
with no effort on his part the words which would be right; but
he was sure that by 'thinking prayerfully', in the 'attentive presence of God', about those words which seemed to him to be best
he would be able to come closer to preaching with a sense that
these *were* right for him to use—and what is more, he could
commit them, along with his own admittedly inadequate and
deficient effort, to God so that they might be used in a way
pleasing to God and more likely to find acceptance from God's
people.

In a book whose topic is the preaching of the gospel, it would
not be appropriate or necessary to speak at length about the
devotional life of the preacher of that gospel. None the less, a
few words may be useful on the subject. Certainly every priest
or pastor worth his or her salt will be one who himself—or
herself—seeks to live as a Christian disciple; and that means
having the habit of prayer and meditation. (Incidentally, I have
regularly added 'her' or 'herself' because I am convinced that
sooner or later the Christian churches, both Catholic and Reformed, will be obliged to recognize the role of women, not least
in the ordained ministry. All arguments, whether biblical, theological, or of any other type seem to me to be mistaken, sometimes based on surprising ignorance, and usually merely an
expression of masculine prejudice!)

One way into a brief series of comments on the devotional
context for the right preaching of the gospel is found in considering seriously the words that are used at the ordination of a
clergyman. As myself an Anglican, I shall use the words that are
found in the Alternative Service Book of the Church of England.
Similar language is employed in other such ordination services,
whether in the world-wide Anglican Communion or in other
Christian denominations.

In the English Alternative Service Book (pp. 356 and following), the bishop who is ordaining candidates for the priesthood
is directed to speak in this fashion in what is called 'The Declaration'; which is then followed by questions and answers intended to demonstrate the reality of the ordinands' 'call to
ministry':

'A priest is called by God to work with the bishop and with
his fellow priests, as servant and shepherd among the people to

whom he is sent. He is to proclaim the word of the Lord, to call his hearers to repentance, and in Christ's name to absolve, and to declare the forgiveness of sins. He is to baptize, and prepare the baptized for confirmation. He is to preside ay the celebration of the Holy Communion. He is to lead his people in prayer and worship, to intercede for them, to bless them in the name of the Lord, and to teach and encourage by word and example. He is to minister to the sick, and prepare the dying for their death. He must set the Good Shepherd before him as the pattern of his calling, caring for the people committed to his charge, and joining with them in a common witness to the world.

'In the name of our Lord we bid you remember the greatness of the trust now to be committed to your charge, about which you have been taught in your preparation for this ministry. You are to be messengers, watchmen, and stewards of the Lord; you are to teach and to admonish, to feed and to provide for the Lord's family, to search for his children in the wilderness of this world's temptations and to guide them through its confusions, so that they may be saved through Christ for ever.

'Remember always with thanksgiving that the treasure now to be entrusted to you in Christ's own flock, brought through the shedding of his blood on the cross. The Church and congregation among whom you will serve are one with him; they are his body. Serve them with joy, build them up in faith, and do all in your power to bring them to loving obedience to Christ.

'Because you cannot bear the weight of this ministry in your own strength but only by the grace and power of God, pray earnestly for his Holy Spirit. Pray that he will each day enlarge and enlighten your understanding of the Scriptures, so that you may grow stronger and more mature in your ministry, as you fashion your life and the lives of your people on the word of God.

'We trust that long ago you began to weigh and ponder all this, and that you are fully determined, by the grace of God, to give yourselves wholly to his service and devote to him your best powers of mind and spirit, so that as you daily follow the rule and teaching of our Lord, with the heavenly assistance of his Holy Spirit, you may grow up into his likeness, and sanctify the lives of all with whom you have to do.'

I have ventured to quote this in full, because it can be useful for those who are familiar with this charge to read it again, while for others it provides an admirable outline of what Christian ordained ministry both means and establishes. Of course the language of the Alternative Service Book lacks the oratundty and elegance of the similar 'exhortation' in the old Book of Common Prayer; but it says the same things in a more contemporary idiom and speaks directly to the persons who hope to serve in the ministry.

It will be noted that great stress is put on the personal devotion of the minister. Prayer to God is an imperative, both for strength to perform the duties which are laid upon such an one and also for the insight and understanding of the gospel of which he or she is to be a representative and a spokesman. Above all, as he or she seeks to 'grow stronger and more mature' in ministry, he or she is to 'labor to fashion [his or her] own life and the lives of [his or her] people on the word of God'—that is to say, on the gospel of God's act in Jesus Christ. And the proclamation of that gospel, along with presiding at the celebration of the Eucharist, is said to be central to the ministry which is being undertaken.

Perhaps I need not say more on this subject, save to urge again that the Ordinal is very clear about the way in which the minister's own life of prayer and meditation is intimately related to all of the duties and responsibilities which attach to that ministry. The point surely is that unless an ordained person is a convinced and practicing Christian, the performance of those various functions will be less than right; 'only by the grace and power of God' received through earnest prayer can those functions be properly exercised. We also observe that the end or purpose of preaching, quite as much as of the other things to be done by the ordained person, is to bring the people to what the older Prayer Book Ordinal called 'ripeness' in Christ—a sharing, to the limit of each Christian's possibility, in the life which is lived 'in Christ' and which is then to be 'witnessed' to 'the world.'

In the course of this exhortation, much is said about 'the word of God' and about the 'understanding of the Scriptures.' This brings us to the subject of the next chapter, which is about the Bible, the tradition of which the Bible is a part, and the relation of both to the Christian proclamation. But before we come to that subject, one final comment seems to be indicated. That comment has to do with the manner in which the ordained person, and in the context of this book the preacher, looks at himself or herself and at ministerial activity. The danger is that it is always possible to be altogether too much concerned to emphasize one's own place and person in this exercise.

When I was young, brought up in what was called 'the High Church' tradition, I often heard priests speak about *their* Eucharist or Mass. It did not dawn upon me until much later how wrong was such an expression. In other traditions, I gather, something of the same sort was thought and said, so that one could hear clergymen speak as if their preaching was in fact *their* preaching. Language of that sort was surely not intended to be presumptuous or blasphemous; it was only a careless way of speaking. Yet it is sadly wrong and improper. As I have said, that it was this only dawned upon me in after-years, as I became more and more certain that ordination does not confer a status but authorizes a function. There was a day when those who had been ordained might easily think that they had been given a very special status as between God and humanity; after all, the sort of world in which many people believed was a world in which such matters of status were familiar and acceptable. Whatever may have been the case at that time, however, no longer can we entertain any such view of the world; nor can we think of ministry in this fashion. I have discussed this at an earlier stage in this book.

The ordained minister who understands correctly what ministry in *Christian* terms signifies will therefore have a certain deep humility as he or she thinks about the office entrusted in ordination. Whatever is done by one who is ordained, is not done instead of but on behalf of the wider ministry of the Church of Christ. It is done representatively, for and in the Christian community. If that is true, then it is done also and ultimately for the Lord of the Church himself. It is as if God in Christ were preaching, celebrating the sacraments, absolving and declaring forgiveness, visiting those who need help, and everything else that is proper to the ministerial task.

So a priest cannot speak or think of *his or her* Eucharist; a preacher cannot speak or think of *his or her* preaching, *his or her* sermon, *his or her* proclamation of the 'good news' about

God's decisive action in Jesus Christ. Of course it is he or she who does the actual celebrating and the preaching; it is his or hers hands, voice, vocabulary, gestures and the like which are the necessary finite human means through which the thing is being done. Yet he or she will bear in mind, sometimes with vivid awareness but (since after all an ordained person *is* human) more frequently as an ever-present but often only vaguely felt sensibility, that God in Christ, God defined by and enacted in the event of Jesus Christ, is the doer, the speaker, the preacher, the pastor, the absolver, the helper. At best the one who serves in the ordained ministry is an unprofitable servant of God. At the same time, however, God deigns to employ human agents and to use human instruments for the accomplishment of his purpose.

In an older theology this would be described in terms of what was known as 'the principle of incarnation' or 'the sacramental principle': that is, things divine are expressed and made known in and by things creaturely. We may not wish to use that idiom today, although there is much which commends it as still valuable and suggestive. But whether we prefer to use some other fashion of speaking or are content to use the older idiom, the basic truth remains constant. It is that basic truth which ought always to be part of ministerial equipment, as we may phrase it.

The exhortation which I quoted in full had several significant references to the Bible and to the Holy Scriptures. I noted this in my comments immediately following the quotation. To that subject we shall turn in the next chapter whose title is 'The Bible, the Tradition, and Preaching.'

The Tradition, The Bible, and Preaching

THERE CAN be no doubt that for centuries the Bible has been not only the major source-book for theological development in the Christian tradition but also—and more immediately relevant to this book—it has been the point of reference for the proclamation of Jesus Christ. Before the New Testament was put together, from the oral traditions about Jesus and the letters and other material known in the primitive Christian community, appeal was made to the Old Testament, that is the Jewish Scriptures, for predictions of and a way for interpreting the significance of Jesus. For this reason, it will be disturbing to some readers when I say that in my view, and I think in that of all informed persons in the theological world, the basic point of reference is the tradition itself. The Bible is part of that tradition but by no means all of it. This theme will be developed in the present chapter.

Protestant and Reformed denominations have tended to regard the Scriptures in isolation from the ongoing tradition of the Church. On the other hand, pre-Vatican II Roman Catholics tended to see the Bible and 'Tradition' (capitalized to indicate the great stress put upon it) as equally authoritative, although in our own time that Council's bringing the two into a unity has made considerable difference. Among the Eastern Orthodox, who in this respect as in so many others seem to have adopted a more appropriate position, the Bible is seen in the fashion I have just indicated as the proper one for us today: as part of the

'holy tradition' of the Christian Church, to be read in the light
of that tradition and not taken in separation from it as a unique
and independent source-book for Christian faith. All this has
had its affect upon preaching. The so-called 'conservative evangelical' in one way and the 'liberal Protestant' in another way
have been so dependent upon the scriptural material that they
have regarded it almost as if it had been dropped from heaven;
like 'Topsy' in the negro story, it has been taken as if it had no
parentage and no association with anything else.

One of the strangest phenomena of our own day has been the
reappearance in so many parts of the world, especially in North
America of course, of a biblical literalism which is very similar
to the 'Fundamentalism' which was prevalent in the United
States during the first few decades of this century. There are
some distinguished and competent thinkers and writers in those
circles, to be sure, but by-and-large the support for it has come
either from ignorant laypeople who find its authoritative manner of speaking emotionally appealing or from those who belong
to what might be called reactionary conservatism and who are
annoyed by much that is found in the modern world and eager
to return to 'the old time religion.' One of the reasons for this is
doubtless the fear that freedom is a dangerous thing and can
lead to all manner of abuse and error. Erich Fromm wrote a book
about 'escape from freedom', in which he noted that for a great
many people this constitutes an escape which they welcome
because it delivers them from the need to think for themselves.
To turn to the Bible and find in it an answer to all possible
questions is an easy escape; many take it. I have been horrified
to see how in a university setting some of the best students in
the natural sciences want just such an infallible authority for
anything not done in the laboratory. When a question is raised
which for most people demands careful thought and responsible
personal decision, people like that will very often simply quote
a passage from the Scriptures, frequently in no way directly
relevant to the matter under discussion and when relevant only
valuable in the context of another age and under other conditions than those which are ours today.

But I need not continue in this vein. There *is* a problem here;
it is inescapable and must be faced and answered. That problem
is simply how in our own day we can use the Bible intelligently

and responsibly, not least in the work which is the preacher's in proclaiming the meaning of the originating event of Christian faith. In attempting to look at that issue I must begin with a very brief summary of what has happened to the Bible, thanks to a hundred years of careful critical study by experts who have brought to their study all the resources available, including linguistic, historical, literary, and many other types of knowledge.

After many years of historical criticism, in which the interest was in dating the various pieces of biblical material, there came literary criticism, in order to establish the relationship between these pieces—in the New Testament especially with respect to the four gospels. Then there was a detailed study of the 'forms', the smaller bits which have been put together in the various biblical books to form some semblance of unity. More recently, redaction criticism has become almost an industry, with attention to the presuppositions, the understanding of faith, and the editorial activity of those who combined things more or less in their present form. Now we hear much about 'canonical' criticism, whose purpose is to see why and how the given material has been used to establish a series of 'authorized' or 'canonical' books which the Christian Church has accepted as constituting the Bible as we know it today. If the reader is not acquainted with this long period of study, with its agreements and disagreements as found among scholars, there are scores of relatively popular works which will provide the necessary information.

For our purpose the important aspect is simply that in view of this long period of investigation we are able to look at the Bible in a much more intelligent fashion, without assuming that it is 'all of a piece'. Hence it is possible to do what Pope Pius XII urged in his encyclical *Divino Afflatu:* to read history, where it is present, *as* history although written of course in the fashion thought right at the time; and to recognize and study poetry as poetry, legend as legend, myth as myth, moral teaching as moral teaching. There is perhaps some surprise that it was a Roman Catholic pontiff who put this so plainly and commended it so earnestly, without for a moment denying the proper authority attached to 'Holy Writ.' What he said was of course familiar in non-Catholic circles for a long time; yet the way in which he said it, with the consequences of that pronouncement in his own communion, is an indication of a growing consensus about the right place and real significance of Scripture in the Christian tradition. Note that I have just written 'in the Christian tradition.' For the truth is that while the Bible and more particularly the New Testament gives us an invaluable mass of material about the formative period in Christian history, it does not stand alone. Liturgies, collections of prayers, theological statements, moral teaching, and much else are included in the general and developing tradition of the Church. The Bible, because it is concerned with the formative period, has a certain normative quality which the Christian centuries have both recognized and employed as a way of discovering continuity in faith, worship, and life, a continuity which has its special focus in what was set down from the oral traditions which told how Jesus was 'remembered', and in the light of the experience of his Spirit (I am using here a valuable point made by Professor John Knox in several of his books about the New Testament and the early Church) revealed the way in which the post-resurrection community understood and handed on what it had been taught.

In consequence, we can now see that what we have in the New Testament is what I have called throughout this book 'the witness of apostolic faith', while the Old Testament has its particular Christian significance in giving us the background of the event of Jesus Christ in the religious faith, worship, and teaching about God's will and way in the world as these were set forth in the Jewish scriptures which then became part of the Christian Bible. This apostolic witness is the basic datum with which the preacher has to deal. It may be possible, although always with uncertainty and the need for modification, to get behind that witness; but this is much more an exercise of biblical scholarship than directly relevant to the task of the preacher —or, for that matter, the work of the Christian theologian.

I have argued elsewhere that the preacher like the theologian must begin with this apostolic witness. But he cannot stop there. The tradition has gone on through the centuries and whatever else may be said about it that tradition is inescapable. It gives us today a continuing awareness of how the importance of Jesus, as I have put it earlier, has been interpreted and related to the rest of the knowledge men and women have had about themselves, their world, and their destiny. Furthermore, the Christian community exists in the contemporary world in which

Christian people have their own specific experience and grasp of what this tradition, grounded in the apostolic witness to the originating event, can mean to them. Thus the preacher always must bear in mind that he or she is not simply 'expounding the Bible'; he or she is also working with the development of Christian faith down the centuries and with the fashion in which that faith speaks directly to people in our own time. This task is very demanding; and that is why it is so necessary that the preacher be informed, so far as this is possible for him or her, about what has gone on in the past, quite as much as what speaks meaningfully to present-day thought and experience.

I am sure, for my part, that the sort of approach which is required in the light of what has just been said gives to the Bible a value that was not known in an earlier time. The necessity for working along such lines is not something to be regretted, although unfortunately many conservatives seem to feel this about it. Rather, it is to be welcomed with enthusiasm, precisely because it makes the scriptural material so much more readily comprehensible. This is another instance, although with extended application, of the truth of Benjamin Jowett's famous comment in the middle of the last century that if we read the Bible as we would read any other collection of ancient writings, we shall find that it is *not* just like any other collection. On the contrary it has its own specialty, because when it is so read we are made sharers in the earliest witness and are brought to grasp that witness more adequately and intimately.

In what sense, then, can we talk about 'the inspiration of the Bible?' Here we shall profit from following the thought of R. P. Hanson, who in several recent essays and one or two books has urged that talk about 'inspiration' has come to be very problematical for us. But the Bible remains, he says, *irreplaceable* precisely because it gives us that primitive witness and brings us to the point where we must decide whether or not we can and should accept as our own the reality which is there set forth. Granted that we may not find the terminology once used very attractive; granted that we must engage in our own interpretation in the light of the rest of the tradition and with due regard for contemporary experience and understanding, the total impact of the Bible is not shaken nor is its essential contribution to the Christian development of faith, as also of worship and moral discernment, to be thought to be in question. Thus the preacher need have no hesitation in doing what he or she was exhorted to do at ordination: apply himself or herself to the study of Scripture, so that the deepest reality of the abiding gospel may be grasped and conveyed through proclamation to the men and women to whom that proclamation is addressed.

I wish now to give an account, inadequate because of necessary brevity, of what the biblical story as a whole has to tell us. Here is what Karl Barth has taught us to consider a great 'saga', but one that is not fictional nor imaginary but grounded in happenings in the world and in the manner in which those happenings were seen and expressed through a long period from the earliest days of the Jewish people down to and through the specific occurrences in Palestine which are associated with Jesus Christ.

We begin with the very early days. Jewish tribes wandered in the desert regions of Arabia and thereabouts, rather like the Bedouin known to us today. They worshipped local deities whose dwelling-places were on hills, at springs, in oases, and other 'holy' places; they were plainly polytheists. As years went by, they came to think that there was a chief among the gods, whom they called Jahweh. He was not the only divine reality but he was *their* god who revealed himself particularly in wonderful acts, such as earthquakes, storms, tribal warfare, and the like. For centuries, probably, this went on. Then a group of these Semites wandered into Egypt, where they were put in bondage and made to do manual work for their Egyptian overlords. They suffered oppression yet they had no way of securing their freedom. But there appeared a leader, known to us in their inherited tales as Moses. With him as their spokesman, they sought release from their bondage; and when this was not given, a band of them fled from Egypt, with militia in pursuit. At some spot where they were obliged to cross marshy land, they managed to get over without harm but their pursuers were mired and gave up the chase.

As the years went by, these tribesmen came to believe that their god, who was superior to all other divine beings, had brought about their deliverance. He was a god of power, who had previously shown himself in 'mighty acts' but who now had crowned all these by a great deliverance for his chosen people.

As a god of power, then, he was a god also concerned for justice; the Jews' cause was indeed just and they had been delivered from oppression and pursuit through what they believed to be his intervention. For some considerable time they wandered about in what was probably the Sinaitic peninsula; then they began an invasion of Palestine, which was not too remote from their former haunts. By a slow process of penetration, represented in their saga as much more a single expedition of conquest, they entered Palestine where they found a distantly related population who long before had occupied that land. This population still worshipped gods in high places and shrines; the gods were the *baalim*, who were responsible for the fertility of the rich land which they inhabited but were also the gods concerned with human fertility. Hence the worship had about it a somewhat sexual aspect which horrified the invaders.

During their slow conquest of Palestine, the religious ideas of the Jews were influenced by what went on in Canaan, as they called Palestine. It was a place to which their god had led them and it was their task to bring him and his cult to a position of dominance. None the less, the Jahweh who had been primarily the god of storm and marvel, as well as the god who was their strong defender, came to be interpreted as also the god of 'seedtime and harvest, summer and winter', as much the lord of the ordinary forces of nature and life as the god of catastrophic action. The process of assimilation went on, with a gradual supplanting of the *baalim* by Jahweh; and in the end the god of the Jews entirely supplanted the non-Jewish deities. What had begun as a sort of polytheism went through a stage of henotheism (one god as *their* god, without entirely denying the existence of other deities), until at last a genuine monotheism was established. This was largely through the so-called prophets, charismatic leaders who were devoted to Jahweh, spoke on his behalf, condemned any alien deities, and labored to establish him as the one and only god with whom humankind had to deal.

What was more, the god who had been concerned with justice in defending the Jewish tribes was now seen as interested in justice within and among the people whom he was believed to have chosen as his own. They were in 'covenant' with him; their conduct must be a reflection of his purposes and must manifest equity, honesty, right dealings, and the rejection of everything that was contrary to his holy will. At this point we may see not only a genuine monotheism but an *ethical* monotheism.

With much back-sliding, which was disobedience to Jahweh and which merited divine punishment, there was nevertheless a slow development of purer and more exalted notions of Jahweh and his character and activity in the world. Later prophetic voices began to speak with even more vigor about the divine righteousness. And that righteousness was interpreted, in such great figures as Jeremiah, Hosea, and the two or three men whose oracles have been put together in the Old Testament book we call Isaiah, as resting back upon and expressing the divine *chesed*—the faithful loving-mercy of Jahweh not only for his own people but for all the peoples of the earth. The entire story is given to us in the Old Testament material, including as it does much genuine history as well as a good deal of legend and myth, not to speak of poetic expressions of the relationship between Jahweh and humankind but with reference also to non-Jewish races and nations.

In the suffering which followed from invasions by Assyrians, Babylonians, and finally by Romans, with an interlude in which there was a Greek hegemony under the successors of Alexander the Great, this Jewish religious faith was enriched and deepened. It reached its highest expression in the prophets just mentioned and in the hymn-book of the Temple in Jerusalem, the Psalter. It also found in synagogue-worship, in which in the towns and villages the people gathered on Saturdays to praise their Lord and to receive instruction, a more direct and intimate religious awareness than had been possible in the formal Temple-worship at the central shrine in Jerusalem.

Out of this long-developing background and in the context of the highly ethical Judaism of the latter part of the pre-Christian period, there appeared another prophetic figure. This was Jesus, a man from the north in Galilee. Jesus taught and acted for the God of his own people. In what he said and did there was an expression both in word and act of the 'faithful loving-mercy' of Jahweh. His very person was later remembered as having been an embodiment or an enactment of that *chesed.* He spoke about and he acted for Jahweh as sheer Love; but the Love which Jahweh was must be understood as adamant and demanding as well as gracious and forgiving. After a period of about thirty years, Jesus was arrested by the leaders of the people and tried before them as a blasphemer; evidently he had spoken about God in so familiar and intimate a manner that these leaders were scandalized and regarded him as a threat to their position and authority. Handed over to the occupying Roman authorities of the time as a rebel and as one who imperilled the peace and good order of the land, he was put to death.

This was not the end of the story, however. Those who had been his disciples were convinced by what they took to be 'infallible signs' that he had been raised from death by God. Others were drawn to the company of the disciples and within a very short time there was a new community which eventually was called 'Christian', since its members were 'the Messiah's flock', so to say. Soon some of the leading men of that company traveled into the surrounding Graeco-Roman world, chief among them of course Paul of Tarsus. Within the space of twenty or thirty years, the 'good news' about Jesus was being proclaimed in many parts of the Roman Empire. And with this spreading of the story, inevitably the philosophical and religious ideas prevalent in that Roman world were employed to interpret the significance of this Jesus and what had been accomplished through him. It is this whole complex of fact and belief which we have reported to us in the apostolic witness. However various were the attempts to speak about him and his achievement, the essential assertion was that in the event of Jesus Christ, they were sure there had been a decisive and focal disclosure of the divine reality known to the Jews as Jahweh and to others under various more Greek and hence more philosophical terms.

What it came down to was the proclamation that in what had happened in and through the Man of Nazareth and Calvary was a vivid disclosure of the one God and a powerful release of that God's power in the world. What Jesus had said and done not only told others about God; it was a human existence, in all its integrity, in which God had acted and wrought, so that within a hundred years, at the most, Jesus himself was described as an act of God. In him divinity and humanity were genuinely united; his human existence was the *organon* (as Athanasius later put it in the early years of the fourth century) for God in the outgoing world-ward expression of the divine reality.

From that point on, the Christian tradition has dared to assert boldly that the event from which it took its origin is indeed marked by both speciality and decisiveness. In the idiom which grew up in Christian theological circles and was widely accepted—after a long period of discussion and controversy—Jesus was styled the incarnation of God and the means by which atonement or deliverance from sin and death was made possible for humankind.

I do not apologize for this lengthy—although in fact far too brief—retelling of the saga which the Bible presents to us. For it is this whole story which brings us to the momment of decision. The Christian proclamation is based upon it; it is, indeed, a way in which that proclamation is given both historical grounding and contemporary relevance. But of course it raises problems. It is with some of those problems or issues that the next chapter will deal, always in the context of the preaching which is so integral to the continuing tradition of Christian faith, worship, and life. And that tradition dares to insist that the story which I have been telling in its human and historical shape is the other side of another story—the story of God's unceasing concern for and activity in and upon the created order and more especially for, in, and upon the men and women whose existence is in that created order.

Problems in Preaching

I N A well-known passage, St. Paul speaks of the 'offense' of
the gospel. What did the Apostle mean in saying this? Certainly not that the gospel is intellectually offensive, even if
it was nonsense to the proud Greek mind and absurdly wrong
to the Jewish mind—to the former it spoke mistakenly of the
personal loving-kindness of God for humans; to the latter it was
preposterous to think that somebody who had been crucified
and therefore condemned by Jewish religious teaching could be
so important as to be called Lord, Saviour, Life-bringer. What
St. Paul was saying was quite different. He was insisting, as
Rudolf Bultmann has emphasized in discussing Pauline thought,
that the gospel of God's generous love enacted in Jesus Christ
offends human pretension to self-sufficiency, human sinful
pride, and human dislike for being recipient of divine grace
rather than able to earn by good works an eternal salvation.

All this is relevant here because it indicates clearly that there
is nothing irrational in the gospel of Christ. It may and it does
affirm what goes beyond the capacity of human speculation or
enquiry; but it does not render human understanding and the
attempt at discovering meaning in existence a wicked or presumptuous exercise. When the Petrine writer urges that we
should be 'ready to give a reason for the hope that is in us', he
is commending those who are prepared to use their minds to
help others grasp what the Christian proclamation has to tell
them.

If the gospel is an offense to human sinfulness and pretension, it can also be difficult to accept, not least in our own day, because it raises questions that are inescapable and that must be met and answered in order to make that gospel speak directly, compellingly, in St. Paul's sense as an offense to sinful men and women as they are, and with the human need to comprehend (in however limited a fashion) what it is about and how it is indeed relevant to their situation. In our day, it seems to me, there are certain intellectual 'problems', as we may call them, which require our attention. A responsible preacher will acknowledge these matters and will seek to handle them, both before he or she ventures to proclaim the gospel and also in the course of proclamation—the latter because unless somehow it is demonstrated in preaching that they are seen to be there as unnecessary obstacles, they may prevent people from facing up to the genuine 'offense' which the gospel inevitably presents. I single out five issues, among the many which might have been chosen, and I shall say something about each of them.

The five major 'problems' which I believe require attention are these. First, whether the event of Jesus Christ is entirely unique and unparalleled in human relationship with the divine —in other words, in what sense ought we to speak of the speciality of that event or (in the more usual way of phrasing it) 'the uniqueness of Christ'. Second, whether we are to regard that event as intrusive into the world so that it constitutes a divine intervention in history or should see the event in a context which relates it more intimately to the wider activity of God in the affairs of history. Third, the question of 'the miraculous' and the meaning which can be given to that concept in a world such as we believe ours to be. Fourth, the presence of many other religious traditions or faiths in the world, brought home to us so vividly thanks to travel, the interchange of ideas, and the increasing realization that this is *one* world. And fifth, the secularization of so many areas of human existence, which makes many wonder if the idea or experience of 'the transcendent' can have any meaning at all. I believe that each of these, however differently it may be expressed in words, is a genuine difficulty for a great many men and women of good-will. Each of them constitutes an obstacle to acceptance of the gospel unless what have become conventional (even traditional) ways of dealing with it are modified in the light of a deeper awareness of what the gospel *really* affirms, on the one hand, and what we know to be the facts about ourselves and the world in which we exist, on the other hand. That is why I have selected these five and shall now proceed to comment on each of them, and at some length.

That there is some special quality about the originating event of Jesus Christ is an inevitable corollary of the importance which is found in it and which the proclamation of the gospel is concerned to affirm. We have talked in an earlier chapter about the focal position of this event in Christian tradition and in the experience which it conveys; we have said that in this tradition and for that experience the event is decisive. We have also used the word 'speciality' to make this clear. But the question is then posed: in what sense, or how, are we to understand this particular quality?

Obviously this is in many ways an issue for theology rather than for preaching as such. Yet it is a very real issue and much in preaching will depend upon how it is answered. I wish to make two or three suggestions which may be helpful in this connection.

First, whatever is said about Jesus Christ cannot so separate him and what he has accomplished in the history of humankind that he becomes, as it were, a 'surd' in the picture. In the early history of Christian thought, there was a continued emphasis upon the genuine *humanity* of the Lord, at a time when it seemed much easier to talk about his *divinity* without stressing the human-ness which was his. To counteract this, the Cappadocian Fathers used an oft-quoted phrase: 'What has not been assumed cannot be redeemed.' This was by way of insisting that only in genuinely human terms could the 'salvation of man' be accomplished; otherwise, anything that might be said would have no immediate relevance to the human condition. We may extend this insistence by saying that if the event of Jesus Christ is *so* alien to human nature and to what men and women have come to know of God and God's more general activity in the world, it will be without context and, what is more, it will be unidentifiable as an act of God at all. The English writer Evelyn Underhill expressed this by noting that unless we have *some* notion of what it means to talk about divine doing and presence, we have no possibility of identifying Jesus Christ with such doing and presence; we are seeking to explain the obscure by the more obscure and are bound to come up with nothing.

In the second place, there is no way in which we can *demonstrate* or *prove* that there is such a speciality about the originating event. To affirm it is a matter of faith. But it is not blind faith, because it rests back upon what has been experienced through a response to the event itself. In other words, it is what traditionally is known as 'the work of Christ' which furnishes the basis for anything that may be said about him as it were 'in himself.' This is significant, because at least in the context of a Process conceptuality 'a thing *is* what it *does'*, as Whitehead put it; what we are talking about, in anything said about the event, is what God *did* there and what 'stream of influence' has resulted from that doing.

Third, the Process conceptuality helps us here by its emphasis on the fact that any and every event or occasion in the world has a genuine special quality. Nobody and nothing can be identical with anything or anyone else—past history, present moments of decision, and future aims are different for each, even if there is a conformity for all of them to that pattern of advance which is integral to the whole creative process. You are you; I am I; John is John; and Mary is Mary. We all meet, we all belong together, we all influence and affect each other; yet we are specifically ourselves, with our own identity as such. The claim for the event we indicate when we say Jesus Christ may be interpreted along those lines. And if the results of the event, in what the 'stream of influence' has come to signify and produce, have an importance which in Christian faith is grasped as decisive for those who are caught up into it, then we may very well proceed to claim that the degree of speciality in that instance is much greater than that which belongs to less important moments.

To say this leads at once to the second major issue, which has to do with a supposed 'intrusion' or 'intervention' of God in that event, without parallels with or intimations present in the wider process. I am obliged here simply to *deny* the necessity for any such notion. Indeed I believe that to talk in that fashion is to come close to denying the divine omnipresence altogether. There is no need for God to 'intrude' or 'intervene' in the world, as if from outside it; in fact, there is no meaning in saying this. Why? Because to speak of God at all is to speak of the ever-present, ever-active divine reality in, behind, and through whatever occurs. God then is *here* or God is *nowhere*, which latter notion is to say that God does not count in the ordinary course of events and that the created order gets on, not very well perhaps, without the divine presence and action. From any theistic view, that is absurd and incredible. Those who talk about 'intrusion' or 'intervention' are probably unconsciously *'deistic'*—that is, they subscribe to the position taken by the so-called 'deists' of the seventeenth and eighteenth century who accepted God as creator in a remote past but were content to think that the creation could now get on without God, although God might now and again interfere with the creation. Otherwise God was still remote and unknown. *Or* they are using unfortunate and misleading language to indicate what earlier in this discussion we have termed the decisive or focal or special quality that Christian faith has discerned in the originating event. In either case, the implications are extremely unfortunate. They suggest that Jesus Christ is so unrelated to what is going on in the creation that he is indeed a 'surd'; we might even say that he is a monstrosity without possible comparison. Then he cannot provide the clue or disclosure of what God is always 'up to' in the world; he cannot reveal, to put it simply, that God's everlasting nature and operation is a Love that is 'of one substance with'—of the very same quality and kind as—what is seen in the Christ-event. That event becomes a complete anomaly.

I believe that these two issues have enormous importance for the effective preaching of the Christian gospel. I need not spell out that importance since it seems obvious. If the event of Jesus Christ is special in an entirely unique sense, so that it has no parallels anywhere, and if that event is so intrusive that it does not illuminate what is going on in the creation by God and under God, then the proclamation of the event is a vain series of words, speaking to nobody and providing no insight into who God is and what God does. Hence it is of no interest, save as a form of words which years ago may have been found valuable but today offer nothing to men and women in their present concrete situation, with their desires and yearnings, their deficiencies and their needs, and their vague but genuine sense that human existence possesses significance and value.

Still another problem which faces a preacher is the question of miracle. What is one to make of such reported incidents if one is not prepared to accept what I have just called a 'deistic' view of God's relationship to the created order? For those who do take that view, whether knowingly or unconsciously, a miracle is an intrusive act of God in the natural world; it is a 'violation' of the order of nature. But in the world view which I have been defending as the only one possible for us today, that sort of understanding of the miraculous can make no sense. On the other hand, it may be that the concept can have a real meaning; and incidently, this may not be remote from the fashion in which miracle seems to be suggested in the biblical material.

In the New Testament, there are three Greek words which our older translators have put into English by the use of the one word 'miracle.' There is *semeion,* used primarily in the Fourth Gospel; its proper translation would be 'sign.' So the verse following the story of the wedding feast at Cana of Galilee would read, 'This is the first of the *signs* which Jesus did; and his disciples believed in him.' In that gospel each miracle-story is associated with a discourse, with the statement of some implicit significance which explains what the tale is really concerned to show. The second New Testament word is *dunamis,* whose correct translation is 'a power' or 'an energy'. And each of the occasions to which this word is applied has to do with a release of God's activity such that it made a difference to those in the story. Somehow in the incident there is a working of God through Christ which brings healing or renews faith or opens up a novel possibility. Finally, there is the Greek word *terrha* (found only in Matthew's gospel, by the way). This word, which comes closest to the 'vulgar' meaning of miracle in later usage, is to be translated as *wonder* or *marvel.* It has to do with what has produced astonishment, surprise, sometimes a sense of awe or worship.

In the New Testament period and of course in the Jewish history which preceded it there was no knowledge of 'laws of nature'; there was only a sense that God's activity in the world had a purpose or objective, which might at this or that moment be vividly disclosed with the consequence that those who wit-

nessed it or heard about it were more profoundly aware of the
reality of God's working in the world. The interpretation of
miracle as sheer intrusion, as the breaking of nature's established order, and the like, is a much later position of which the
biblical writers would have known nothing.

I have said again and again that God's working in the world
is by 'acts of love'; that God *is* Love and that God's doings in
the world are ways in which that divine Love is operative. Now
I propose that we can best understand the genuinely *religious*
significance of the stories about miracles in those terms. To use
the New Testament words, here stories are told which have to
do with ways in which God was disclosed through signs of the
loving divine activity, in which there was a release of the divine
power which is love, and in which men and women were
brought to marvel at exactly such disclosure and release. Of
course we cannot know exactly what took place in any of the
many reported incidents; the preceding chapter was intended to
show that our way of seeing the Bible leads us to regard those
incidents not as sheer reporting, as might occur today, but rather
as witnesses of or testimonies to faith in God through the event
of Jesus Christ. The stories told of Jesus' 'mighty works' are a
reflection of the primitive Church's own faith and are intended
to awaken in those who hear or read them a similar faith. Hence
I say that the point of the stories is not to assert anything like
that which the 'vulgar' notion of miracle might suggest but to
bear their witness to the conviction of the first Christian disciples that in and through the happenings which together make up
what I have so often styled the event of Christ, there was indeed
a disclosure or sign of divine love; there was indeed a release
of divine power in love for the wholeness of human existence;
and there was indeed a demand that in the presence of this
disclosure and release the believer be brought to give God
praise and glory as he or she wonders or marvels at just such
a reality. I believe that it was the Anglo-Scots philosophical
theologian A. E. Taylor who once wrote that in the presence of
the miraculous in the New Testament sense we are brought to
say, 'Oh! my God!' Those who are theologically informed will
recall here that the German theologian Schleiermacher said
much the same thing: that a miracle in the biblical way of under-

standing it is any event which evokes religious faith both in God
and in God's presence and action in the world.

The preacher can use these stories without necessarily sub-
scribing to their historical accuracy; he or she can speak about
them and direct attention to them on the part of those who hear
the proclamation, as indications of the speciality of the event of
Jesus Christ, in its disclosure of God's nature and activity and
in its 'letting loose into the world' the divine energy of love. The
preacher can help contemporary Christian believers to read the
biblical material with this point as central, compelling, and
evocative of a deeper faith in God. In a similar fashion, the story
of the virginal conception of Jesus, found only in Matthew's and
Luke's gospels, will be a way in which witness was given to that
same speciality; or, in another way of phrasing it, the virginal
conception narratives are not concerned with the biological
question of Jesus' conception and then his birth but have to do
with the conviction that it was indeed *God* who was in and
behind the coming to live amongst us of One who was both
entirely and genuinely human but also and for faith supremely
was part of the divine activity to bring men and women to share
in the divine Love. In respect to the resurrection narratives in
all four gospels, we can say once again that the point is not in
attempting to reconcile the patently diverse material on the
subject with whatever may have been the supposed residual
historical fact; but rather it is to show that although Jesus had
truly died on the Cross, that was not the end of him. He was so
much the enactment of divine Love that 'he could not be holden
of death'. The reality of that divine Love enacted in the event
was so enormous that nothing could stop it. God received into
the divine life this human enactment while at the same time it
was so released into the world that those who had known the
Lord Jesus in 'the days of his flesh', and those who through their
witness were led to respond to him, could and did experience
'new life in Christ' and were empowered to work for him in
continuing his mission of 'amorization' in the affairs of the
world.

If anyone should say that what has been argued in the last
few pages is a 'reduction' of the historic faith and hence inadequate as a context for the right proclamation of 'the Word', my
reply is simply a flat denial. Far from being that, it is an attempt,

however successful or unsuccessful, to *maintain* the historic
faith in the light of undeniable developments in biblical understanding and with honest acceptance of our present way of
seeing the world in relationship to God. The discussion in the
last chapter about the Bible, the tradition, and Christian preaching had for its chief object making clear that the only way in
which we can properly affirm the faith which the Christian ages
have professed is by what Pope John XXIII called *aggiornamen-
to,* which does not mean 'reduction' but does mean our coming
to see the faith in terms which are intelligible to our own time
as well as appropriate to the apostolic witness which is given
in the Bible and supremely in the New Testament.

The Anglican Articles of Religion asserted that nothing is to
be held as part of Christian belief save that which can 'be
proved—which in the days when the Articles were composed
meant 'tested'—by 'most certain warrant of Holy Scripture.' I
should claim that what we have been saying stands up to that
'most certain warrant', once those writings are correctly understood and properly interpreted. Far from being a 'reduction',
therefore, what has emerged is a re-affirmation.

There are two other issues with which we shall concern ourselves in the present chapter. One has to do with the non-
Christian religions, about which we now have a much more
adequate knowledge; the other has to do with the omnipresent
phenomenon of 'secularization', found in all parts of the world,
both in the older countries and in the 'newly-developed countries' wherever they may be.

In an earlier day, people had no genuine acquaintance with
most of the non-Christian religions, save for Judaism and to a
certain extent Islam. Nowadays we are aware of and most of us
have a deep respect for Buddhism, Hinduism, and even for the
more 'primitive' religions. Very few people, even among conservative groups, are likely to dismiss all these as instances in
which 'the heathen in his blindness' is thought to 'bow down to
wood and stone.' There may be much in them that we find
difficult, perhaps mistaken; yet we are not ready to say that they
are nothing more than ignorant and entirely false attempts on
the part of humans to construct their own religion on the basis
of sheer superstition, total error, and a disregard of the one and
only God there is—for there can be but *one* God, despite the

variety of approaches and interpretations of deity found among
humans. The day of what Arnold Toynbee once bitingly condemned as 'Christian imperialism' is long past, save perhaps in
some back-woods sects and among absurdly reactionary
groups.

In the early Church the great thinkers were by no means guilty
of that imperialism. By differing devices, theological and practical, they sought to show that 'the Word of God', the *Logos,* had
been made known through divine providence to all men and
women; while they were also ready to say that this 'spermatic
Word', diffused throughout history and down the ages, had sup-
plied enough of the truth for those who accepted the non-Christian faiths or the philosophies which in some cases took the
place of religious belief so that God had never 'left himself
without witness.' What was particular and special about Christianity, they said, was that in Jesus Christ this 'diffused' Word
was (as they put it) 'made flesh' in a distinctive and special
manner. We may prefer other kinds of statement but the point
is clear: The main tradition of Christianity has been much more
generous, 'hospitable' in Baron vonHugel's word, to these different non-Christian faiths than many have thought; yet this has
been without for a moment surrendering the conviction that in
Jesus Christ something decisive is to be found. I cannot attempt
here to develop this approach, not only because I am insuffi-
ciently instructed in the non-Christian faiths but also because
to seek to work out the newer position would require a book in
itself. Suffice it so say that there is a great benefit for the preacher in being able to recognize that God is somehow in touch with
all men and women, that their 'salvation' is in God's hands not
in ours, and that our task in what used to be called 'the mission-
ary enterprise' is to share with others that which is so important
and so dear to us who believe in Jesus Christ. Thus the preacher
can boldly affirm with Archbishop William Temple that we
need only believe that the work and the person of Jesus Christ
are both the completion and coronation of all the divine working
in the world and also the correction or error or misunderstanding. Christian faith is not the outright denial of what in other
religious traditions has been said about God and humanity—or,
as in some varieties of Buddhism, about the fulfilment of human
possibility even if God is not named or worshipped in the con-

crete circumstances of men and women anywhere and every-where.

Finally, I shall say but a few words about 'secularization', since already by implication and occasionally by explicit comment I have indicated what I take to be a right Christian attitude. The increasing secularization of life does not amount to a totally secular—that is, non-religious and entirely humanistic—position. Bonhoeffer's remarks, already noted, are to the point here. Insofar as secularization is an insistence on human dignity and human responsibility and a refusal to make God into a universal panacea for all human ills, we can welcome it gladly. Only when it is given a totally secular expression does it constitute an enemy of Christian, and indeed all other, religious faith.

For the preacher the important thing is to affirm that God is everywhere at work; and where God is at work, the God who is there active is the same God who is known and adored in his distinctive and decisive presence in Jesus Christ. Perhaps one way of making this plain to our contemporaries is to urge that when and where goodness is sought and to some degree found, truth is sought and to some degree discovered, justice is sought and to some degree established, health and abundance of life are sought and to some degree made available . . . in so many ways and under so many 'secular incognitos' God is carrying out his great purpose of love. Thus, to repeat what has been said in earlier parts of this book, the clue or key to what God is always 'up to', always doing, always evoking from humanity, always providing for the sons and daughters of divine Love, is to be seen, known, accepted, and implemented in what we as Christians dare to say has been declared in the event from which our Christian faith took its origin and to which it always returns: namely Jesus Christ, whom we believe to be the Lord and Saviour whose 'name is above every other name'—and all this is 'to the glory of God the Father.'

At the end of the last chapter, I spoke about two 'stories.' One was the historic and human story whose outline, with many detailed incidents, is to be found in what the Bible has to tell us, coming to its culmination in the event of Jesus Christ and its immediate consequences. The other story was the story of the divine initiative and activity which Christian faith has discerned in the historic and human story. The two stories are different and yet Christian faith has believed them to be truly *one* story, seen from different angles and understood in different terms. That they are indeed one story cannot be demonstrated. How could the historic and human *demonstrate* any such thing? It is with that historic and human story that the scholars and biblical critics and historians necessarily deal. But the witness of faith, based on the facts of experience and the experience of facts, need not be alien to nor contradictory of the interpretation which the tradition has given it. Perhaps I may be permitted to claim that the conceptuality which I have used in this book helps to make the tradition's claim more probable, although of course not inevitable.

In the following chapter we shall turn to some of the religious affirmations, both theological (or about the God-world relationship) and moral (or about how faith and life in faith entail a pattern or principle of human existence) which in the Christian tradition have been seen as basic. For the proclamation of the gospel these affirmations provide a background, never to be obtruded but always present; and for a preacher, aware of his representative function and rightly informed about the thought of the past which is still effectual in the present, these are matters of the highest importance.

Preaching, Theology, and Ethics

PREACHING IS not a theological exercise, as if the preacher were delivering an informed lecture on the subject. Neither is it an exercise in moral teaching, as if the preacher were only discussing the best way for human living. I have already made this point and I shall not labor it again. Yet it is equally necessary to remember that all sound and proper preaching, when done responsibly by the one designated to proclaim the 'good news', has its theological and moral presuppositions and consequences.

For this reason I shall now proceed to set down what seem to me to be the basic convictions which are affirmed in the Christian tradition. The discussion which follows is not intended to be complete; it is suggestive and fairly brief, yet it is concerned to make plain what the agelong Christian tradition, the 'social process' which is the living community we call the Christian and Catholic Church, has come to believe. The task of theology as such is to give as coherent and consistent an account as is possible for the finite human mind, of what faith entails. In the language of the middle ages, *fides qua creditur* —the continuing act of believing—leads to *fides quae creditur* —'the faith' by which the community lives and which it believes to be as true as any such human statement can be. There has been development, to be sure, but it has been continuous with the past and seen to be relevant in the present. So also with the subject called morality. The specifically Christian emphasis is upon what is implied and suggested, even demanded and required, if the affirmations of 'the faith' are taken with utmost seriousness. Once again there has been development. But also once again there has been a continuity of past and present; once again there is the conviction that here is something which is relevant to the lives of men and women today as in earlier days. So let us now proceed to set forth those basic convictions and the moral consequences which they are said to entail.

First, as I have urged again and again in our discussion, *God* is at the center of the theological enterprise, precisely as God is at the center of a working Christian faith. God is 'that than which no greater can be conceived', as Anselm phrased it; as such God is the supreme reality, living and active and loving. What the ancient compline prayer calls God's 'eternal changelessness' is not a matter of a supposed metaphysical immutability and impassability; rather, it is a matter of the utter faithfulness of God, the divine dependability, the divine resourcefulness, the divine excellence. This God, who is the one and only God, is above and transcendent to the creation—inexhaustible and beyond our human grasping. This God is active within the creation, enabling its response to the divine intention —here is the divine immanence. This God is also alongside the creation too, disclosed by act in the affairs of the world; here is what I like to name the divine concomitance. And 'the nature and name' of this God is nothing other than sheer Love, personally related to the men and women who are God's beloved children.

Second, those who are God's beloved children are made, or rather are being made, toward the divine image. They are being created out of the materials of the world to become reflections of the divine Love and to serve as personalized instruments for the working of that Love. As such they are *good.* But tragically they have persisted in seeking their own ways and hence are in defection from their intended nature—they are 'sinners.' Through millenia of wrong decisions, with the inevitable consequences of such choices, they are now in a situation where their potential goodness cannot be realized as it should; what is more, each one of us, of himself or herself, continues to choose wrongly. Hence the situation is the more aggravated, the more serious, the more irremediable. But to human existence in its inadequacy and defection, God comes in the ceaseless love which *is* God, to remedy this and to bring people into a right relationship with God and with other humans. In human freedom, they may respond to this action toward them; or they may fail to respond. Yet God still cares and works faithfully for their return—as embodied creatures, compounded of matter and spirit, whose wholeness is always a possibility for them.

Third, in the event we name when we say 'Jesus Christ', God has acted in a focal way, so far as we humans are concerned, both to reveal the reality and pervasive action of divine Love and to release into the world of human affairs the power of that Love for the re-making of human existence and for its establishment in the divine purpose. In a fully human life, lived among us and sharing with us the conditions which are ours, God has acted. In that event there is a coincidence of the prevenient Love which is God and the responsive human loving which is potential in each of us. The models often used to describe this have been unsatisfactory, to be sure; talk of 'substance' has led to much confusion and misunderstanding, as has talk of the union of wills or the association of divine/human consciousnesses. What is really being said is that divine activity and human activity are at work—always and everywhere, to be sure, but that in Jesus Christ these two 'come to a point', so that the latter can properly answer to and serve for the former. God acts first and then there is the human response, the human 'Amen' to the divine initiative. The result is a decisive exhibition of how things are meant to be—for even if humans had not sinned, this would have been the divine purpose for humanity. Here is no incidental nor accidental occurrence; but a culmination in what I call 'the classical instance' of what always and everywhere God is 'up to' with human existence.

Fourth, through that focal event, there is both a disclosure of God in the integrity and inexhaustibility of the divine loving *and* the 'letting loose' into human experience and history of the divine power (or 'grace') which enables a right response to be made and which establishes in human existence the reality of life in love with other men and women, so that human society may become more and more the place where 'the works of love' are performed and where justice, deliverance from oppression, and rightness of relationship are given the chance to be effectual

within the inevitable limitations of a finite creation. This is
'redemption', not as if it were merely a rescue from human
failure but as an indication of and an empowering for the
'wholeness of life' (*shalom,* as the Hebrew has it) which God
purposes for men and women both in their personal existence
and in their social belonging.

Fifth, human destiny is not exhausted by life in this finite
world where we live out our days. The final destiny of human
existence, as of all else in the creation, is *in God.* Into the divine
life things creaturely, including the human agents in the world,
are received and accepted and find their abiding meaning. The
book of our human life comes to an end, in one sense, when we
die—as die we all must; but that is not a final stop, since in God
there is precisely such reception. The happenings in the creation
are valued by God; they are important to God; they make a
difference to God and in God. In the deepest Christian insight,
whatever idiom may be adopted to state this, God and world are
so related that each affects the other. God does not become
more divine, of course; but God has other and more varied
opportunity to adapt the divine Loving to the creatures, so that
in any and every circumstance there is the renewed possibility
of novelty, with the emergence of a greater capacity to act
instrumentally for God's intentions in the world.

How this 'reception' is accomplished and with what degree of
conscious awareness of it on the part of the creatures we do not
know. But exactly because God is unfailingly Love and unfailingly loving, we can have the confidence that God will do the
best which can be done—and that best will be the fulfilment of
creaturely potentiality and the enactment of divine purpose. In
God, 'where moth and rust' cannot damage or destroy, all that
is salvable *is* saved; what is more, it is used by God—not as if
it were a way of divine self-exaltation but for the true 'glory of
God', which is self-giving at its fullest and best. If Philip Larkin's
fine words about *An Arundel Tomb* (that what remains after
death is our loving) are the truth—and something deep in human
existence affirms that they are—then what matters most of all
about any one of us is the way in which and the degree to which
we are enabled to contribute, however imperfectly this must
seem to us, to the delight of God and the implementation of
God's will and way in the world.

We are judged or appraised by how we have made this contribution. Our destiny is to be *in God* but whether this is negative
or positive will depend upon the openness of the human person
to the divine Love and the expression of that Love in and
through the affairs of our daily living. Hence there is an accountability which no human can evade.

Sixth, the divine working is universal, not confined to the
human level of existence. The 'whole creation' is the sphere in
which God is active, in most various ways and in different
degrees of intensity. Hence the Eastern Orthodox emphasis on
the cosmos, in its entirety, as having a place and part in the
working-out of God's intention is entirely right and proper. It is
too bad that an almost incurable anthropocentrism has marked
so much of our western ways of theologizing that we have
tended to do less than justice to the other aspects and areas of
the creation which are not directly related to the human enterprise as such. Obviously we cannot know how this cosmic operation is effected but we can at least make sure that we do not
'parochialize' the divine love and talk as if its only interest is in
what happens in the realm of human affairs. The creation at
large is not simply a stage upon which the one significant drama,
namely human life, is acted out; on the contrary, it is *all* significant so that the very 'stars in their courses' are important and
have their place in what God is doing in the creation.

Seventh and last, such considerations lead us to see that
when we speak of the divine creativity we are not pointing
toward a single historical event 'at the creation', as if that were
past and done with. God is ceaselessly creative; the world is
continually 'being made' and we humans are part of that 'being
made', with our own genuine freedom, our own dignity, and our
own responsibility to play our proper role in the enterprise. If
this implies that God has always 'had a world' in which there
is divine activity, that does not mean that the creation is 'necessary' to God, as if the divine existence could not be conceived
as transcendent over and unexhausted by what goes on in that
created order. Yet because God is Love, there must be relationship in deity such that *some* creation is involved in the total
picture. To speak of a Creator without a creation is to talk
linguistic nonsense—quite as much as to speak of creaturely

freedom as if it were a freedom apart from dependence upon God's initiating and continuing concern.

Here we can see that the Genesis story of creation, like the Revelation account of 'the end', is to be taken as a way of saying that as all has proceeded ultimately from the divine Love, so all is in the end directed to the divine Love. From that Love a creation has been brought into existence and continues to exist; toward the further enrichment of the divine Love the creation is intended to make its own contribution. Otherwise, the creation is a pointless and unimportant affair. But with this understanding, the creation has its significance and its value; because it 'matters' to God, it 'matters' also in itself as a sphere in which God finds worth and in which God exerts the loving energy which is the divine character or nature.

I quite realize that what has been said in these seven points is an inadequate and doubtless defective account of what Christian theology at its best has been concerned to affirm. Each point might have been expanded; each of them also needs, what there has not been space to provide, a defense against criticism. Furthermore, some of our inherited theological formulations do not measure up to and may on occasion seem to contradict the account which I have just given. Nevertheless I am convinced that what has been said is on the right lines and that it provides a kind of summary of the best insight and interpretation in the theological tradition which we have inherited.

For basically what we need is an illumination of the concrete data of lived religious faith. We cannot hope to have a 'chart correct of things in heaven and earth.' To assume that we could have such a chart is to presume too much; it is to be guilty of that *libido sciendi*, 'lust for knowing', which Jacques Maritain quite rightly has condemned as one of the worst manifestations of human sinfulness. On the other hand, since we must say *something*, we can properly seek the best possible in making sense of and giving sense to the profound reality of the Christian life in grace, lived out in the context provided by the ongoing historical tradition which is the Christian community of faith. We should acknowledge always the imperfection of our statements yet be ready to trust the *communis sensus*, the 'agreed sensibility', which is at the heart of our concrete Christian existence. We can say *something*, even if we cannot presume to say everything. And what we do say must in some fashion be appropriate to the witness of the Christian centuries and also available or intelligible to men and women who live out their lives in today's world.

On occasion one may be asked to put down, in a even briefer fashion, what is basic to the Christian theological and moral perspective. I recall that Wystan Auden once told me that when asked to do just this during a lecture-series which he was delivering at an American university, he replied by reciting the Nicene Creed! That was clever and in the circumstances perhaps appropriate. But of course the creedal statement, hallowed as it is by centuries of use during the celebration of the Eucharist, can be understood only when it is seen as a combination of supposedly historical data, theological affirmation put in a quasi-philosophical idiom, and a good deal of symbolic language (with the use of such phrases as 'came down from heaven', 'ascended into heaven', and the like). My own proposed summary of course lacks the creed's historical freightage and is hardly the sort of thing that may be *sung*, say to the plainsong *Missa de Angelis* or *Missa Marialis* tones! Yet for what it is worth and with the conviction that it may speak meaningfully to men and women today I should now say something like this:

"We who are Christians commit ourselves in confidence to a supreme Love that is personalized, creative, and sovereign in the world. We affirm that this divine Love was enacted in the human existence which is central to the originating event of the Christian tradition, in the rich totality of that existence. For us this is the sufficient and compelling symbol of what and who the cosmic Lover truly is and what that Lover is "up to" in the world. This Jesus lived among us as truly human; he died and was buried. Yet he "could not be holden of death", because the human love which was his was taken into the divine life and there abides for evermore. Knit together in a fellowship of response to this enactment of divine Love in Jesus Christ, we belong to a communion of men and women which is a unity, which is for all people, which is integrated and enduring, with a mission to proclaim its faith to the world. In this assurance, we believe that our human destiny is to be received, like him, into the divine life, to be used of God for the furthering of the divine purpose in the creation.'

If that summarizes what I take to be the theological perspective, the moral perspective follows as a necessary consequence. That can be expressed much more simply and directly—and in words that the New Testament attributes to Jesus himself: 'You shall love the Lord your God with all your heart and soul and mind and strength; and you shall love your neighbor as you love yourself.' Obviously those brief words need to be spelled out in more detail. Yet their main drive is clear enough. The moral consequences of Christian faith are to be found in the urgent desire for and dedication to such loving. To say this entails also such concern for, such seeking and striving after, and such commitment to work toward, the reign or rule of love in the hearts of men and women and in the worldly affairs which inevitably must be theirs. All of which is to the end that there shall be justice and righteousness in human society, deliverance from oppression and from the negation of human potentialities, and the establishment among us of harmony, sympathy, understanding, and concord, both in our personal and our corporate existence.

The End of Preaching

I N THIS book we have discussed various aspects of the preaching of the gospel or the proclamation of the 'good news' about the originating event of Jesus Christ, as I have consistently called it. We have seen what this gospel or 'good news' consists in; we have looked at the people to whom it is to be proclaimed; we have considered the preacher and the setting in Christian worship in which the proclamation is normally made. We have said something about the place of the Bible in the living Christian tradition which preachers represent and for which they function; we have discussed a few of the problems or questions which are raised both for preachers and for people; and we have tried to sum up the theological and moral implications of the gospel as these have been worked out in the tradition down the centuries. Now we come to our final chapter. It has to do with what I have styled 'the end of preaching.'

As I noted at the beginning, when I sketched the way in which we were to proceed, the word 'end' has two meanings. One has to do with the goal or final conclusion of whatever matter is being considered; the other has to do with the purpose or intention which is in view. Thus when we speak of 'the end of man' we can be looking at his death and whatever may lie beyond death *or* we can be indicating what that instance of humanity is here for, what is the purpose or meaning of life, what each one is aiming at in what is said and done. The same sort of distinction may be made when we are talking about the proclamation. Hence we shall first look at the purpose or intention of the preaching of the gospel. Then we shall attempt to see what is supposed to take place when the proclamation has been made— when the sermon has been delivered to the people present. To what point or conclusion is that preaching supposed to lead, so that when it is done and over, there may be a situation or circumstance which has been, so to say, the 'end-product' of the enterprise?

I turn then to look at the purpose or intention which the one who proclaims the 'good news' will have in view as he or she prepares what is to be said and who then goes on to say it in the context of an act of worship.

When the preacher mounts the pulpit to deliver the sermon, something must be in mind. What is it that this preacher hopes and prays will be accomplished as the proclamation is made? Obviously there must be some purpose, if what is to happen is other than a talk or lecture or address on an important theme. A responsible preacher will want the sermon to bring about some significant result which will be appropriate to the message and meaningful to those who listen. I believe that we can sum this up by speaking of repentance, commitment, and service; and I shall say something about each of these.

One purpose of the preaching, then, is to awaken repentance. But what is that? First of all, it is not an emotional revulsion about oneself and one's doings. That would be what traditional penitential theology calls 'attrition', which is a profoundly disturbed state dependent largely upon a given individual's psychological-physiological make-up. Some may have this but it is not the important matter. That latter is what the same penitential theology calls 'contrition'—a genuine sorrow for the ways in which one has failed to live up to the possibilities that are hers or his; and hence a sorrow for a failure in relationship with God and one's fellow-humans—for these two are not contradictory, as some seem to assume, but are two sides of the same coin. To fail to be one's true human self is to fail in maintaining on one's part the right relationship with God in the divine intention for mankind and *at the same moment* a failure in right relationships with other men and women and children, characterized as it should be by the caring, sharing, giving, and receiv-

ing which brings about a condition of peace and concord—
which is *shalom* or abundance of life.

Contrition is accompanied by a resolution to alter all this, so
far as one is able to do so. It means *metanoia* or a conversion
of one's intentions and aims so that they may become those
which are proper to genuine humanness. Such repentance, with
the wish for a forgiveness that looks toward the future and is
not merely regret about the past, is awakened when the gospel
is authentically proclaimed. It is not that repentance precedes
an awareness of acceptance and hence the opening of new
opportunities; rather, it is that when one knows through the
action of God in the event of Jesus Christ that one is already
accepted and forgiven by God the great Lover of the world,
one's only response can be, 'I am unworthy.' *Because* I am
already and always accepted by God, who is the One 'to whom
all hearts are open, all desires known, and from whom no se-
crets are hid', who knows each of us better than any of us can
know ourselves, *then* I am impelled to see my own inadequacy,
defects, failures, and wrongs. And I am also impelled to turn, or
to wish to turn, to the right ways.

If a sermon does not have this as one of its purposes and
accomplish this as one of its consequences, then somehow it has
not been the authentic proclamation of God's disclosing and
delivering action in the event of Jesus Christ.

In the next place, a purpose of proclamation is to bring about
genuine commitment, whether this is for the first time (as with
some who are present it very well may be) or is a renewed
response in self-dedication to God who in Christ has acted
decisively for us humans and for our wholeness. Once again,
such commitment, primary or renewed, need not be a matter of
strong emotional reaction. That will depend, as does the act of
genuine repentance, upon the particular psychological-physiological condition of the hearer. With some there may be an
almost overwhelming sense of being caught up into a new life;
with others, probably with the majority, it will be much more a
matter of decision and purpose that is not highly-fevered but is
rather a strong determination to give oneself fully and un-
reservedly to the Lord and to that Lord's work and way in the
world.

A sermon which does not have this for a major purpose and

which fails to awaken some such response among those who are present is a sermon which might be described as 'short-circuited'; its authentic quality is either missing or is diluted so that it is not effective. No preacher can avoid this judgment. The 'value' (if that is the right word) of the preacher's speaking will be determined precisely by the degree to which it has or has not brought about a first commitment or a renewal of commitment.

Then, in the third place, the proclamation has for its purpose more than a momentary commitment or even the wish for a long-term commitment. It includes a challenge to the listeners to give themselves, to the best of their ability, to the discipleship which is service of God among humanity—to 'do the works of love', with as much of the self's devotion as can be managed. Here is exactly what one of the thanksgiving prayers in the Eucharist asks: that we 'offer God our souls and bodies, to be a living sacrifice', which means that we know ourselves to be 'sent out to live and work to God's praise and glory.' It is not enough to say as sincerely as we are able, 'Lord, Lord.' We must also do what that Lord commands. And an authentic proclamation will intend that result.

Now it is obvious that none of these purposes of the sermon will be achieved perfectly or even adequately. This a responsible preacher knows very well. Yet there can be no excuse for that preacher's failure to do all that is in his or her power to bring men and women to 'ripeness' in Christ, as the old Ordinal phrased it, and thus to be brought into a way of living which is both enabled and enriched. Set in the context of the Eucharist, this tells us that the words of the other thanksgiving in the Alternative Service Book are to become real: 'May we who share Christ's body live his risen life; we who drink his cup bring life to others; we whom the Spirit lights give light to the world'; and with this there go the final words of that prayer, 'Keep us firm in the hope you have set before us, so we and all your children shall be free, and the whole world live to praise your name; through Jesus Christ our Lord.'

The over-arching purpose in awakening repentance, establishing commitment, and requiring God's service in the world, may be accomplished through a number of what I may style 'sub-purposes.' In the preaching of the gospel, there are many opportunities, such as the following of the 'church year' will

suggest or that will seem otherwise appropriate at a given time
or place. At Christmas, for example, the main emphasis will be
on the coming of God to the world, supremely for us in Jesus
Christ; at Easter, the stress will be on the victory of God's Love
in Jesus Christ over sin and evil and death. At Pentecost, the gift
of the Spirit with new life in Christ as its accompaniment will
be the central theme. So we might go through the 'church year'
and see that the various lections which are appointed for each
Sunday and for festivals or times of special observance suggest
the particular aspect or element in the proclamation which will
be appropriate and desirable. This gives a richness and variety
to the preaching, bringing out fresh ways of declaring the loving
and delivering activity of God. There is no reason to assume
that uniformity and sameness are required; the event of God in
Jesus Christ is so 'many-colored', as used to be said, that stale-
ness is likely only when the preacher himself is stale and the
preacher's grasp of the essential proclamation has become tired
and hackneyed.

As I have been writing this last chapter I have been thinking
again and again of the splendid way in which Charles Wesley's
hymns set forth both the authentic gospel *and* its infinite variety.
In that great hymn, 'Come, O thou Traveller unknown' (which
Wystan Auden and T. S. Eliot both considered one of the finest
religious lyrics in the English tongue), the basic gospel proclamation is given: 'Pure universal Love thou art: to me, to all, thy
mercies move: thy nature and thy Name is Love.' The hymn, 'O
thou that camest from above' is a prayer that God's glory shall
bring those who have seen it in Jesus Christ to 'work and speak
and think for [him]', so that each believer may 'prove [test]
God's perfect will', repeating the 'acts of faith and love', and
when death comes be enabled, because death 'seals God's end-
less mercies', to make 'the sacrifice [of self to God] complete.'

There is another hymn by Charles Wesley which is very much
to the point here: 'O for a heart to praise my God!' I quote in full
the last three short verses:

> A humble, lowly, contrite heart,
>   Believing, true, and clean,
> Which neither life nor death can part
>   From him that dwells within:

* * *

A heart in every thought renewed,
   And full of love divine:
Perfect and right and pure and good—
   A copy, Lord, of thine!

Thy nature, gracious Lord, impart;
   Come quickly from above;
Write thy new name upon my heart,
   Thy new best name of Love.

To awaken the urgent desire to pray such a prayer is the purpose of all authentic Christian proclamation.

Perhaps enough has been said about the purpose or intention of the proclamation. In doing this, we have also seen how one of the consequences of authentic preaching is a determination, established in the hearts and minds and wills of those who have assisted at worship, to give themselves more fully to the service of God—as 'co-creators', in Whitehead's fine word, with God in the great work of 'amorization', establishing in this world (so far as a finite order will permit it) a society marked by caring, justice, responsibility, interest in others, and relief from oppression, devoted to everything positive which promotes the fullest actualization of human possibility. But we must be brought to understand that along with such dedication to service or to work, there is another 'end'—in the sense now of that which comes when the proclamation has been made and there has been repentance for wrongness, commitment to God disclosed and the divine power of loving released in the originating Christian event, and when the imperative to service has been accepted and implemented in action.

What is that 'end'? I believe that it is the bringing of God's human children to worship and adoration. As those words are commonly interpreted this may suggest a static and altogether passive matter. As I intend them here, it is the realization of the presentness of God in the world here and now and therefore a genuine participation in the divine life. I must develop this theme.

The old Westminster Catechism opens with a grand statement. To the question, 'What is the chief end of man?' the answer is given that this 'chief end' is 'to glorify God and to enjoy him forever.' In the Roman Catholic popular catechism, a similar response is made, this time to a question asking why one has been created: 'to worship and serve God.' And in Revelation, the New Testament book which in highly imaginative and poetic language portrays the heavenly city, we find once again that worship is the dominant theme.

If we engage in the 'de-mythologizing' of the Revelation to St. John the Divine, as we must also 'de-mythologize' the creation stories in the book Genesis in the Old Testament, we realize that what is being said is that as human existence and the world in which that existence is set has its origin in the circumambient, everlasting, faithful Love that is nothing other than God— we recall Wesley's hymn, quoted a few paragraphs back, that 'his nature and his Name is Love', and Dante's great closing line in *The Divine Comedy* about 'the Love that moves the sun and the other stars'—so also the 'end' toward which all creaturely existence moves is that very same Love. The biblical story is a great symphony, whose opening is the announcement of the major theme, the creative love of God in action, and whose grand finale is the magnificent and triumphant re-affirmation of the same theme. The whole story is, as it were, a love-story with God as the principal actor and the human creation called to participate in that adventure of Love at work. What can such a presentation do, save to bring men and women to their knees in adoration and praise?

Worship and work go together, as the American religious philosopher William Ernest Hocking so well put it in his book *The Meaning of God in Human Experience.* The Benedictine motto is *orare et laborare,* 'to work and to pray.' This motto has often been incorrectly quoted, as if it said not *et* but *est*—that 'to pray *is* to work', and conversely that 'to work *is* to pray.' The misquotation, as so often can be the case with such error, happens also to state a profound truth. The highest work is in fact prayer; and all prayer when devoutly undertaken is an activity and not merely a state of mind nor an emotional attitude.

So I would urge that in the labor which a Christian undertakes as part of discipleship, what is required as a motivation and inspiration is worship; while genuine worship is itself something done, with as much of self as the man or woman engaging in it can manage to bring to this exercise of creaturely dependence and humble obedience. Something of what this implies has been suggested in our chapter on worship as the context for proclamation. Here I need only add that in the act of worship there is granted a glimpse of heaven itself.

Yet we need to ask what *is* 'heaven' or (put otherwise) what is the final destiny for us humans? For what do we hope, once we have grasped in worship 'a little bit of heaven?'

Before attempting to answer those questions, it is necessary to make some further comments about what in the historical Christian tradition have been called 'the last things.' Often these have been taken as suggestive themes for the Advent season of the 'church year', although in truth that season is directed rather to the expectation of the so-called 'second coming' of Christ which will bring to a completion that which in the 'first coming' at Christmas was started. Obviously talk about a 'second coming', while intimated in a good deal of biblical material, belongs in the category of mythological discourse and hence presents great difficulty for many called to preach in the Church. Hence the tendency has developed to use the Sundays of the Advent season for a consideration of death, judgment, heaven, and hell —these are the 'four last things.'

The Christian tradition has never sought to evade the reality of human death, neither has it been remiss in calling the attention of believers to their own mortality and the importance of their being prepared to face this inescapable fact. Again, God who is sheer Love must inevitably be also adamant in the requirement that humans shall live so far as they are able in and by such love. Therefore the tradition has spoken insistently of judgment—or to use perhaps a better word, appraisal—both moment by moment and at the conclusion of every human life, with a further appraisal made when the entire created order is evaluated in its contribution or failure to contribute to the advancement of the divine purpose in the world.

Heaven and hell are in the picture as the two possible ultimate destinies for humankind. Heaven is the 'enjoyment' ('fruition', from Latin, is the term often used and its meaning is just such enjoyment) of God which will be granted to those who have been truly obedient to the divine will toward love: Hell is the state or condition of those who have been and done evil despite all the invitations and solicitations of God.

Now it is obvious that we are here in what I have called the realm of mythological discourse, just as much as when there is talk about a 'second coming.' What then *is* intended by our hope of 'heaven'?

Surely the answer is that our hope for heaven is hope *in God*. God, in whose loving reality made known to us in these brief glimpses in the act of worship, gives us 'joy and peace in believing'; and that God is our human destiny itself.

Unfortunately a good deal of popular talk seems to assume that in addition to God we can and should expect rewards which consiously we know to be ours. Often there has been an immoral transaction in view, as in the Victorian hymn, 'Whatever Lord we give to thee/ A thousand-fold repaid will be', with its lamentable concluding lines, 'Then gladly will we give to thee/ Who givest all.' Dean Inge once said in his acid fashion that this sounds more like engaging in a profitable investment in shares or bonds than like anything genuinely Christian. And I might also quote here St. Francis de Sales' appropriate comment: 'We are to seek the God of consolations rather than the consolations given by God.'

We are to seek *God*. God is the end of all our human striving; and to be accepted into the divine life and made forever a sharer in the divine love is the goal or end of which worship is the intimation and the invitation. How that will take place is a matter about which we do not possess information. Yet the Christian trust in God assures us that God will do for us 'more than we ask or think.' In whatever fashion is possible—and God is the God of possibility as well as of actuality—God will do for humankind the best that can be done. What could be better than to be taken into God's own life where Jesus Christ has gone before? That Lord Christ, says the children's Christmas hymn, 'leads us on to the place where he has gone.' And this place is in God, where all that has been accomplished in the creative advance, along with those who have been agents in that accomplishment, are unfailing remembered and treasured, for what they are and for what has been done by them.

Others may wish to be much more explicit about such things; but for my part I am content to leave it there. If God is what has been disclosed in the event to which we look with gratitude and joy, then we are glad to entrust ourselves to our creator, deliverer, and sanctifier. The long process of divine action in the world, with its beginnings in the past—so far as we can talk meaningfully about 'beginnings' at all—has been continued in every present moment and in some fashion will reach its conclusion, although we are unable adequately to think or speak about 'absolute' endings. The creation has its own integrity, its own freedom, and its own responsibility. These God respects, values, and employs; yet it is in God that the point and significance of the creative process is to be found. And the earnest Christian believer knows this and rejoices in it.

Another question can be asked, which has to do with what is commonly called 'personal immortality.' This is a Greek conception, hardly mentioned in the Old Testament and only indirectly mentioned in the New Testament. The earliest Christian way of talking was concerned with 'resurrection.' First of all, it asserted that the central figure in the originating event, namely Jesus Christ himself, was 'raised from the dead' by the act of God, after he had been crucified on Calvary. Then 'in' Christ, the Christian faith has gone on to assert, those who have been made members of 'his Body' will also be raised from death to God. The stories about Jesus' resurrection told in the four gospels are contradictory and impossible to bring into a proper consecutive order; we have already said that this is the case. But what is the reality which the stories are concerned to declare? I believe that the answer here is that God has indeed taken into the divine life the fullness of what Jesus was and what Jesus did; this fullness is forever 'part of God', as we may put it. But for the Christian 'resurrection' means also that this same Jesus, in the Spirit which is central to what I have called 'the stream of influence' which the total event released into the world, is also effectual in the continuing life of men and women, as they are brought to respond to him. In all this, humankind is to share.

In that context, the Christian is ready to entrust himself or herself to the God who is indeed the creator, but also the redeemer and sanctifier. Blessed be he (Jewish and Muslim prayer repeatedly says) in whom we can have complete confidence! We are freed from 'faithless fears and worldly anxieties', to use a fine phrase from the American Prayer Book, and know that 'our chief end' is there, in God and nowhere else. Thanks be to God—and thanks be to the Lord Jesus Christ from whose enactment of the divine Love we have come to know this reality of faith. Knowing this, we know also that everything good and right and just and beautiful and true is safe forever in that same God—to whom be glory and praise, adoration and thanksgiving, for all time and eternity. The establishment of this reality in worship is the 'end' of Christian preaching.